Tom Murphy
Plays: 4

A Whistle in the Dark, A Crucial Week in the Life of a Grocer's Assistant, On the Outside, On the Inside

A Whistle in the Dark depicts the reunion of an Irish family in Coventry: 'A fine, furious play about men trained to anger.' *New York Times*
' . . . it is a considerable, and refreshing, shock to encounter this clenched fist of a play . . . National identity has been a theme in the contemporary Irish drama common to Murphy, Friel and McGuinness. Nothing has been so brutish and direct, though, as this picture of Irishmen "over here" asserting themselves in one of England's post-war dream cities.' *Financial Times*

A Crucial Week in the Life of a Grocer's Assistant focuses on the deliberations of John Joe Morgan, 'pulled between the compulsion to leave small-town Ireland and the desire to stay . . . The play is intensely funny, and there are times when you want to shriek with laughter, but the laughter is of a special kind – it is the laughter of recognition. . . . A devastating comment on the failures of the last twenty years to resolve the dilemma of emigration.' *Sunday Tribune*

On the Outside (written with Noel O'Donoghue)/*On the Inside* are two early plays set outside and in a village dancehall in the 1950s:
' . . . the author transcends period in his treatment, blending sympathy with cynicism of adolescent callowness and vulnerability.' *Guardian*

Tom Murphy's work includes *A Whistle in the Dark, Famine, The Morning After Optimism, The Sanctuary Lamp, Conversations on a Homecoming, The Gigli Concert, Bailegangaire, Too Late for Logic, She Stoops to Folly* and *The Wake*. His career has been markedly associated with the Irish National Theatre (the Abbey Theatre). He was born in Tuam, Co. Galway. He lives in Dublin.

TOM MURPHY

Plays: 4

A Whistle in the Dark
A Crucial Week in the Life of a Grocer's Assistant
On the Outside
(*written with Noel O'Donoghue*)
On the Inside

with an introduction by Fintan O'Toole

Methuen Drama

METHUEN CONTEMPORARY DRAMATISTS

This collection first published in Great Britain in 1989
by Methuen Drama
as *A Whistle in the Dark & Other Plays*
Methuen Publishing Ltd
215 Vauxhall Bridge Road
London SW1V 1EJ

www.methuen.co.uk

Reissued with a new cover in 1993; reissued with corrections 1997

Methuen Publishing Ltd reg. number 3543167

ISBN 0 413 71450 0

A CIP catalogue record for this book is available at the British Library

Typeset by Wilmaset Ltd, Wirral
Transferred to digital printing 2004

Caution
All rights whatsoever in this play are strictly reserved. Enquiries about rights for
amateur and professional performances should be directed to:
Alexandra Cann Representation, 12 Abingdon Road, London W8 6AF.
No performance may be given unless a licence has been obtained.

Contents

Tom Murphy:
A Chronology

Introduction

There are certain times and certain places in which tragedy can be written. Times of great and apparently sudden change. Times when the ground is shifting so fast that there is not one world but two, a past that is melting into the future, leaving a present in which cause and effect break down, in which there is no consonance between intentions and consequences. Places in which this change is still so visible in its entirety that it can be dramatised. And there are writers – very rare ones – who have both the instinctive understanding of the change that is happening and the sense of form with which to embody it, allowing them both to plumb the depths of that tragedy and to transcend it. When these three things – time, place and writer – come together, something extraordinary can happen in the theatre. Ireland and the late 1950s and early 1960s are such a place and such a time. Tom Murphy is such a writer.

Murphy's early masterpiece *A Whistle in the Dark*, written when he was a 25-year-old schoolteacher in a small town in the West of Ireland, is a tragedy written at a time when conventional critical wisdom held that tragedy was dead. For the main centres of English-language theatre, Britain and the United States, tragedy was indeed dead: things were falling apart, for both the theatre and the wider world this was the decade of dissolution and disillusion, of autism and absurdity. The idea that a character or group of characters on a stage could in some sense represent an entire society at a moment of crisis – the idea that is central to tragedy – was simply not on. In Ireland, for very specific reasons, it was on, and Murphy had both the breadth of vision and the ferocious grasp on realistic detail to realise that possibility.

The very specific circumstances in which the four plays in this volume were written are easy to summarise. The first of them, *On the Outside*, is written in the pivotal year in the history of the modern Republic of Ireland: 1959, the first year of the First Programme for Economic Expansion. That Programme, a desperate response to the previous decade which had seen the virtual depopulation of the Irish countryside as young people in their thousands left behind the stagnation, poverty and boredom of Ireland for the bright lights and big bucks of English cities, called for nothing less than the transformation of conservative, rural, agricultural Ireland into a modern, urban, industrial capitalist society. The transformation that had taken place in other western societies over hundreds of years was to be telescoped into less than a decade. In such an inherently dramatic transition, two worlds seem to exist side-by-side for a time, a world of tribal family loyalty, of local piety, of untamed, 'uncivilised' behaviour on the one hand and a world of ordered urban existence, of the nuclear family, of getting on and settling down, on the other. The clash between these two worlds is the material for these plays.

Conflicts like these, of course, don't present themselves to people in terms of programmes and statistics and policies. For someone like Murphy growing up in the small town of Tuam, County Galway, where he was born in 1935, the transition from a largely rural society to an urban industrial one was not a sociological consideration. It took the form of an immediate, traumatic choice – the decision to stay or to emigrate. *On the Outside, A Whistle in the Dark* and *A Crucial Week in the Life of a Grocer's Assistant* form a rough but nonetheless inseparable trilogy whose movement is from emigration to exile to return.

It is no accident, for instance, that both *A Whistle in the Dark* and *A Crucial Week* begin with the arrival or departure of a train, for in Murphy's early life the railway station was the most important and dramatic place in Tuam. As *A Whistle in the Dark* opens, the air tingles with excitement at the impending arrival of a father on a train. As *A Crucial Week* opens a young man in uneasy dreams hears the impatient whistle of a departing train.

The fact that *On the Outside, A Whistle* and *A Crucial Week* do constitute a rough trilogy should be reasonably obvious, but because the plays were not produced in anything like the order in which they were written and have never been seen together, it is a point that has to be made. *On the Outside* was written in 1959 but was not produced professionally until Radio Eireann did it in 1962, and had no professional stage production until 1974. *A Whistle in the Dark* was produced to a mixture of acclaim and notoriety by the Theatre Royal, Stratford East in 1961. But the play which followed it, *A Crucial Week*, though written in 1962, was not produced until 1969. For theatre audiences in Ireland, Britain and America, the plays have never been understood together, as they should be.

The point is much more than an academic one, for it bears on the nature of Murphy's theatre. Murphy is a playwright whose work encompasses tragedy in a way that very few modern writers have managed, but, just as importantly, he is a playwright who moves through and beyond tragedy, towards something quite different: transformation. *On the Outside* and *A Whistle in the Dark* end in blind alleys of entrapment and the latter play moves with all the tragic inevitability of an *Oedipus Rex* or an *Agamemnon*. But – and this is crucial to Murphy's ultimate vision – *A Crucial Week* moves beyond the entrapment, slips the bonds of time and circumstance and demands a changed reality. *On the Inside*, written in 1974 as a companion piece to *On the Outside*, re-inforces this movement by suggesting at least the possibility of freedom for its central characters. *On the Outside* ends with the inevitability of emigration, *A Whistle in the Dark* with the impossibility of escape. Staying at home is not an option. Going into exile is not an escape. The struggle of *A Crucial Week* and *On the Inside* is for the freedom to reject this false choice, the freedom, not to resign oneself to the claustrophobic oppression of small-town Ireland, but to stay in a changed place, a place liberated of its burden of secrets.

On the Outside is a remarkable play in a numbers of ways – in having been written with such a perfect sense of construction and such economy of dramatic language by a young man who had barely seen professional productions of plays, let alone written any; in that within a very simple story and a very short play a whole range of social tensions is dramatised; in the way the mundane story of two young men waiting outside of a rural dancehall which they haven't the money to enter takes on the metaphysical lineaments of heaven, purgatory and hell.

The play works like a metaphysical conceit, yolking together things which should be opposite: love and economics, town and country, a supposedly traditional rural Ireland with the trendy Americanisms of the aptly named Mickey Ford. Theatrically, it works on a simple but very precise irony of inclusion and exclusion. Physically locked out, Joe and Frank are mentally locked in. The place they are trying to enter, the heaven which should lie at the end of their purgatory – the dancehall – looks, we are told at the start like 'a place of compulsory confinement more than one of entertainment'. Being on the outside is bad, but there is no sense that being on the inside would be much better since the play's strongest image of inclusion is Frank's vision of the whole town as a big tank with him and Joe at the bottom, clawing at the greasy walls. There is no way in and no way out. The play's closing line, with its promise of emigration, holds out little prospect of a successful escape: 'Come on out of here to hell'.

Murphy's next play, *A Whistle in the Dark*, surely one of the most remarkable first full-length plays of modern times, dramatises that hell and the impossibility of that escape. Michael Carney has left Mayo for Coventry, hoping to leave behind the tribe, the dark past of history, the whole baggage of sentiment and romance which is merely the other side of violence. His ambitions are the modest, mundane ones of the Ireland of his time: a decent job, a nuclear family, a nice little house, a modicum of dignity and respectability. Michael, to his fingertips, is the new Ireland labouring to be born. But, as surely as Oedipus or Agamemnon he is pursued by the past, a past that is both the flesh of his own family and the soured spirit of a haunted, marginalised people.

A Whistle derives its extraordinary power from the balance between the ferocity of its violence and the classical precision of its form. Kenneth Tynan called the play 'arguably the most uninhibited display of brutality that the London theatre has ever witnessed' and he is certainly right about the play's overwhelming sense of menace. But the impression he creates is false: the violence is not uninhibited and we do not, for the most part, witness it. Those acts of violence which we do see take their effect from the fact that they are short, quick and precise, contrasted to the carefully contained evocations of off-stage brutality. Here is not the stoning of baby carriages, but the slow-burning, intense anger of those who see in violence, not release but duty, not debasement but a kind of ennoblement. Michael Carney is called to violence as Hamlet is called to violence – as a debt of honour, a matter of family feeling. Here violence is an expression of loyalty to a dying feudal code, a commitment to a way of life that believes it can elude urban industrial civilisation in the name of a warped, sentimentalised romance of the past.

In *A Whistle* much of the violence that we see takes on the air of something ritual, something inevitable and therefore shocking only in our realisation that we expected it, that we have been waiting for it. The really shocking violence is the violence of language, the language that Dada uses to control his sons, the language in which Harry recalls the humiliation of his childhood. The most violent image of the play is not to do with knives and knuckle dusters and chains. It is Harry's memory of a teacher searching his hair for lice and fleas, a memory of cruelty and hurt and degradation. This is what makes *A Whistle* a tragedy rather than a brawl, a play about trapped people rather than the racial slur that so many in both

England and Ireland first took it to be.

For all its gritty realism and its deceptive trappings of naturalism, indeed, *A Whistle in the Dark* has much more in common with a Greek tragedy than it has with the kitchen sink drama of the fifties or the absurdism of Harold Pinter, who used it as a direct model for *The Homecoming*. Much of the play reminds us of the Greeks – the story of a house accursed in which the sins of the fathers are visited on the sons; the triumphal return from bloody battles which the Carneys make after their defeat of the Mulryans; the Oedipal tinge in the make-up of Michael, who tries to usurp his father both as protector to his mother and as father figure to Des; the way that the hanger-on Mush acts as a fickle chorus, immortalising the deeds of the Carneys in his bathetic ballad and then cursing them as tinkers. Formally, too, the play preserves the classical unities of time, place and action. That a classical tragedy could be made from the story of a group of Irish thugs in Coventry is a mark of how extraordinary the inherent dramatic possibilities of the Irish situation at this time were and of how masterfully the shaping imagination of Tom Murphy controlled those possibilites.

A Whistle in the Dark is haunted, as so many of Murphy's later plays were to be, by a potent absence, in this case by Mama, the downtrodden woman who never appears on stage but whose image lies at the back of so much of Michael's misplaced desire to preserve and reform his family. In *A Crucial Week in the Life of a Grocer's Assistant*, that absence is filled in. Here it is not an overbearing father with whom the central character John Joe must struggle, but an over-loving Mother. *A Crucial Week* is a comic play which does not ignore tragedy but rather contains and overcomes it. The tragedy of the play is Mother's – the tragedy of a woman caught with the values of one time in the situation of another, the same tragedy of transition which doomed Michael in *A Whistle*. But the play seeks to get beyond that tragedy.

John Joe's own position, caught between the misplaced nineteenth century nobility of his mother and the bitter, despairing fruits of twentieth century material success embodied in Packey Garvey, the emigrant home for the burial of his father, is potentially tragic. The unreality of his situation, caught between one world and another and thus existing in a kind of half-life, is dramatised as much in the form of the play as in the content, as much in the shifting ground between waking and dreaming as in the sociological sense of the new economic order in Mr Brown's bluster about changing times. His plight is as much psychological as it is economic: he dreams of money only as a means to ending dependency, as a passage to adulthood. The struggle in the play is not so much between the necessity of going and the necessity of staying. It is the struggle for the right to make a real choice, the adult right to imagine a changed future and decide to live in it.

The play's stylistic achievement of a kind of never-never land between fantasy and reality is again an entirely appropriate one to its dramatic substance. For the people of the play – John Joe, Peteen Mullins, Agnes Smith, Miko Feely – live in an extended childhood, floating in the unstable mixture of the real and the imagined that is the condition of the child. The feeling of a fairytale that surrounds the play is exactly right, for like overgrown sleeping beauties, its people live in suspended animation, waiting for the magic words, the spell-breaking formula, to be spoken. It is John Joe's achievement to speak those words, conjuring up his hidden brother Frank, telling out the town's secrets, banishing all the festered truths so that they may never have the power to injure again as Mother has injured Alec. Through the power of words, the tragic cycle is broken. The tragic gives way to the magical. It is a break-through that at once encompasses and transcends the way the world is. Few contemporary playwrights have managed so much.

Fintan O'Toole, 1989

A Whistle in the Dark

A Whistle in the Dark was first performed at the Theatre Royal, Stratford East, in 1961 with the following cast:

MICHAEL CARNEY	Michael Craig
HARRY CARNEY	Darren Nesbit
DES CARNEY	Dudley Sutton
IGGY CARNEY	Oliver McGreery
HUGO CARNEY	James Mellor
DADA	Patrick Magee
BETTY	Dorothy Bromley
MUSH	Seán Lynch

Act One

The plays opens on a confusion of noise, movement and preparation. The room and its effects show signs of misuse. There are three doors: one opens to the hall, front door and front room, the second to the kitchen and rear of house, the third to the stairs. HARRY, in vest and trousers, garefooted, carrying his shoes and one sock, is looking for the other sock. He is about thirty. HUGO comes rushing down stairs to go to the mirror and give a liberal dressing of oil to his hair; he is singing snatches of a pop song which appears to hold a personal amusement for him; he is rather stupid. IGGY is fully dressed, waiting impatiently. He is a big man, the biggest in the family, and fancies his image in his good suit. He stammers occasionally – in moments of tension. He affects a swagger when he walks; the swagger is called 'the gimp': shoulders hunched up, one shoulder higher than the other, arms slightly tensed and held out a little from the sides, and thumbs sticking outwards from the sides. This is the walk of 'a tough-un', an 'iron man'. Fighting is an innate part of Iggy's character and is not without a touch of nobility in his case. BETTY is English, about twenty-eight. She enters and exits through the scene, with bedclothes, pillows, etc., to and from the front room.

Generally, all of them are preoccupied with themselves.

HARRY (*looking for sock*). Sock-sock-sock-sock-sock? Hah? Where is it? Sockeen–sockeen–sockeen?

HUGO (*singing*). 'Here we go loopey loop, here we go loopey laa . . .'

HARRY. Now–now–now, sock–sock!

BETTY. Do you want to see if that camp-bed is going to be too short for you, Iggy?

HARRY (*without looking at her, pokes a finger in her ribs as she passes by*). Geeks! (*Continues search for sock.*). Hah? Sockeen.

BETTY. Iggy?

IGGY. Are we r-r-ready?

HARRY (*in frustration*). Stock-king!

HUGO. Maybe you dropped it on the stairs.

IGGY dashes up the stairs. The doorbell is ringing. BETTY going to answer it. HUGO beats her to it and admits MUSH. HUGO and

MUSH *in front hall, in greeting to each other, singing 'Here we go loopey loop . . .'.*

HARRY (*simultaneously, finding missing sock in one of his shoes*). Aaa! Hidey-hidey, was you? (*Drops his shoes with a clatter on the floor.*)

HUGO *and* MUSH *entering.* MUSH *is about thirty, a small fella, cheapish new suit; sycophantic.*

MUSH. 'Allo-'allo-'allo!

HARRY (*sniffing socks*). These has been dead for a year or more.

HUGO. Did you find it?

MUSH. I wasn't long, was I?

HARRY *throws his balled-up socks at* MUSH; MUSH *catches them and throws them at* HUGO; HUGO *retaliates by throwing a cup at* MUSH *which smashes against the wall,* MUSH *shooting at it with an imaginary gun.* BETTY *exits to kitchen.*

HARRY. Easy with the delph –

IGGY (*entering with* HARRY's *shirt which he dumps on a chair*). Sh-sh-shirt. Sh-sh-shirt –

HARRY. Jesus, d'yeh want me to cut the feet of myself! (*He has picked his way across the room to search in a drawer for a clean pair of socks.*)

MUSH. Heigh-up, Ig!

IGGY. T-t-t-train'll be in.

HARRY (*finds clean pair of socks*). Doesn't this colour suit our Michael now? Boghole brown.

IGGY. Harry, t-t-t-train.

HARRY (*there is a hole in one of the socks*). Jesus! Person'lly, my 'pinion, English women is no good, 'cept for maybe readin' real true love stories. (*Calls to kitchen where* BETTY *is.*) Oi! No use English birds.

IGGY. We-we-we ready?

HARRY. No value for money is English flesh.

IGGY (*to* HUGO). Look at the t-t-time.

HUGO. Better run alright. Be (*a*) nice thing for Dada and Des to arrive and we not there.

HARRY. Don't mind selling but person'lly wouldn't be wasting good money on no English charver. Oi, Mush?

MUSH (*picking up pieces of broken crockery*). England, beauty and home, Har.

IGGY *sighs heavily over* HARRY's *perverse slow dressing and is unconsciously thumping the door-panel behind him.*

HUGO. Ever seen a man put his fist through a door?

MUSH. I seen a fella one night –

IGGY. E-e-ever s-s-seen a man open a door without turning the knob?

HUGO *nods in invitation to* IGGY *to try it.* MICHAEL *is heard coming in front door.*

HUGO. Stall it: Michael.

HARRY. Hold on to it (*the door knob*).

IGGY *is holding the handle against* MICHAEL *who is on the other side of the door.* HUGO *is giggling.*

MICHAEL. Betty!

HARRY. Is he trying against you? (IGGY *nods*) . . . Now! Let it go.

IGGY *releases the door handle: the expected* (MICHAEL *to come flying in*) *does not happen. After a moment* MICHAEL *enters. He is in his working clothes – perhaps a boiler-suit which he gets out of during the following scene. He is about thirty-five.*

HARRY. Our Michael would've made a great footballer: that's what's called antic'pation.

MICHAEL. That train will be in now.

IGGY, MUSH *and* HUGO *exit –* HUGO *singing 'Here we go loopey loop'.*
HARRY *putting on his jacket is having some difficulty with the lining in the sleeve, but containing his irritation.*

HARRY. Not coming with us to meet Dada and Des?

MICHAEL. I'll get the beds and things fixed up.

IGGY (*off*). H-h-harry!

HARRY. The beds and things are fixed up. (*Still smiling but thrusts his fist and arm viciously through the sleeve of his jacket.*) Hah?

He follows the others out.

MICHAEL (*calls to kitchen*). Heigh-up!

BETTY comes in and starts to tidy up in silence.

. . . Your slip is – (*showing*)

BETTY. It's clean.

He shuts the front door and returns with a paper bag containing some bottles of beer which he has left in the hall. They look at each other for a moment. Then she smiles at him and shakes her head to herself.

BETTY (*referring to his brothers*). Honestly!

MICHAEL. I got a few bottles of beer. Keep them happy.

BETTY. I still think you should have gone to the station.

MICHAEL. There's enough of a reception committee gone down. They'll be here in a few minutes.

BETTY. Things are going to be cramped.

MICHAEL. It'll be just for a week anyway.

BETTY. Maybe Des would stay on.

MICHAEL. No. Just a holiday.

BETTY. Will your father mind sharing a room?

MICHAEL. Are the beds fixed up okay?

BETTY. Will your father – Well, will he like me, sort of?

MICHAEL. Come here to me, Brummy.

BETTY. The house is really awful. I can't help it.

MICHAEL. No, you'll like Des.

BETTY. I've heard enough about him anyway. When you proposed I thought you'd say, Des and I would like you to marry me – you – us – whatever it is.

MICHAEL. No, you'll like him. He's not like me – I think you'll like him.

BETTY. There will be seven of us for tea. There's only four cups in the house now.

MICHAEL. They all won't want tea.

BETTY. I've eight saucers.

MICHAEL. You can buy some tomorrow. Just Dada and Des.

BETTY. That's all right, but this buying more cups business, and putting in more panes of glass, and –

MICHAEL. Not tonight.

BETTY. What? But isn't it daft? Everything. Look. Just look at the place after a few weeks of family life with your brothers. And now two more.

MICHAEL. Not tonight, Josephine.

BETTY. You what?

MICHAEL (*English accent, joking*). You what? We can drink out of the saucers; it's an old Irish custom.

BETTY. No, it's daft.

MICHAEL. And we'll get a little pig, a bonham, to run around the kitchen as a house pet.

BETTY. Daft.

MICHAEL. And we'll be progressive, and grow shamrocks instead of geraniums. And turn that little shed at the end of the garden into a hotel for the fairies and leprechauns.

BETTY. You're daft. You really are. We were doing pretty well before you asked them here. Daft!

MICHAEL. And we'll –

BETTY (*suddenly serious*). No, I don't think it's small or funny.

MICHAEL. Neither do I.

BETTY. I'm not saying your father and Des aren't welcome, but the others –

MICHAEL. Not tonight.

BETTY. It's all right trying to be the big brother but you're not getting on so well with them, are you?

MICHAEL. Not tonight.

BETTY. Well, when are you going to –

MICHAEL. This isn't the time anyway!

BETTY. I think it's as good a time as any.

MICHAEL. Oh, leave it so, can't you! You're rushing around like mad. Have a rest for a while or something. The place is fine.

BETTY. What?

MICHAEL. The place is fine! Relax, have a rest, I'll give you a shout when they come.

BETTY. Upstairs, is it? That is, if the fighting and crashing all over the place doesn't start. Is it the table or chairs that got it this time?

MICHAEL. Yes – yes – yes.

BETTY. Who will make the bid to sleep with me tonight?

MICHAEL. Don't make a big thing out of it. Harry was drunk that night.

BETTY. Harry is drunk tonight, the others are drunk, they're always drunk.

MICHAEL. Don't start it, for Christ's sake! Jesus, haven't I enough on my mind!

BETTY. All right. Quiet so. But look at it this way: I married you, not your brothers. Since you asked them here we've hardly gone near each other. If I'm on my own here, I'm standing in there (*kitchen*) afraid to make a sound; if I'm upstairs I'm afraid to make a sound. That's just natural, is it?

MICHAEL. Look –

BETTY. That's the way every young married couple is, is it?

MICHAEL. They're a bit wild –

BETTY. Wild? Hah!

MICHAEL. Yes! Wild! A bit wild. They're my brothers, I have a responsibility. It's our family. A bit wild. They never got a chance. They'll change.

BETTY. You're going to bring that about?

MICHAEL. I'm the eldest –

BETTY. Your father is the eldest. What about your responsibility to me? You're married now, you know.

MICHAEL. I know.

BETTY (*silently*). I see.

MICHAEL. Look –

BETTY. Which comes first, which is more important to you, me or your brothers?

MICHAEL. That's silly, stupid talk.

BETTY. Is it? It usen't be.

MICHAEL. Look, what do you think will happen –

BETTY. What do you think will happen to me!

MICHAEL. And with Des coming here now –

BETTY. To hell with Des and the rest of them! It's us or them. Which is more important to you?

MICHAEL *goes out to the hall, opens front door and stands outside for a few moments. He returns to the room.*

MICHAEL. Harry and Mush are coming with the cases. (*He puts his arm round* BETTY.)

BETTY. Maybe you should ask Mush to move in with us too.

MICHAEL. Shhh, Brummy. Your slip is still showing.

BETTY. I don't know.

MICHAEL. It'll be okay.

BETTY *goes into the kitchen.* HARRY *and* MUSH *enter.*

MUSH. Niggers?

HARRY. No.

MUSH. Blacks?

HARRY. No, I wouldn't call them that neither.

MICHAEL. Did they arrive all right?

MUSH. Muslims?

HARRY (*considers this*). Yeh. That's fair. We're Catholics. I got the first good beltin' I got for years off the Muslims a few weeks ago. (*To* MICHAEL) Hah?

MICHAEL. Did they arrive okay?

HARRY. But I still like them. Respect them. Blacks, Muslims. They stick together, their families and all. And if they weren't here, like, our Irish blue blood would turn a shade darker, wouldn't it? (*To* MICHAEL.) Hah? And then some people'd want our cocks chopped off too.

MUSH. One-way tickets back to the jungle for us too, Har, if they weren't here.

MICHAEL. Are they coming?

HARRY. Hah? Dada is looking great, you'll love to hear, Michael.

MUSH. The lousers must have stayed on for another one at The Lion.

HARRY. Des too.

MUSH. He's a Carney all right.

HARRY. Yeh. He's got big, big bones, loose, he'll be a hard hitter.

MUSH. When he learns about the nut.

HARRY (*laughs*). He's learned it. His first lesson, Michael. Half an hour over and young Des has a scrap already.

MICHAEL. What? What happened?

HARRY. Aw! You're awful worried, aren't you? Same as that night with the Muslims. Awful worried, aren't you?

MICHAEL. For God's sake, he's only a kid.

MUSH. He's the biggest kid I ever seen.

HARRY. One scrap already and tucks more on the way.

MICHAEL. What happened? . . . Mush?

MUSH. The train was in, and they were waiting in The Lion, and we were all having a few –

HARRY. Oh, he's no beginner on the beer, Des isn't. I spotted that straightaway. I wonder what he used to do with the money you used send him? Schoolbooks, hah?

MUSH. And Des went out to the jacks and we heard the scuffle starting.

HARRY. No, he's no beginner on the beer. Are you sure you don't mind him bustin' his pioneer pin? Person'lly, I do.

MUSH. And we breezed out lively, Michael, and these two English blokes – one of them putting the nut into Des.

HARRY. Terrible job it's going to be, buying pints for Des and brandy for Dada.

MUSH. But they seen us coming, and they're scappering lively, and Des is dropping, and one of them, you know, shouting, ''e was lookin' for it,' but Hugo got him a right fong up in the arse as he was running out the passageway. And your father was crabbed as hell when he heard they got away.

HARRY. But the place *you* were standing; you could have got the other fella.

MUSH. But I swung, Har, on me oath. Didn't you see me? But he was coming this way – see? – and I had to throw the punch with my right. But, normally, I punch with my left, chop with my right, 'cause I can't straighten this little finger – see? – since my accident.

HARRY (*quietly amused*). Hah?

MUSH (*laughs*). Hah-haa, Har! (*Chants.*)

And Harry struck and Iggy struck
And Hugo struck and then,
Upon the floor, all K.O. dead,
Were the bloody Englishmen!

MICHAEL. Is Des all right?

HARRY. The bloody Englishmen, the lousy Englishmen. And there's a lot of lousy Irishmen too. Isn't there?

MUSH. Scores of them. They're all the same.

HARRY. They're not the same.

MUSH. No, oh no, some are different right enough. Some are tougher, like you and Iggy. It's the –

MICHAEL. Is Des all right?

HARRY. Don't you hear the man talking? (*To* MUSH.) They're not the same.

MUSH. That's what I was going to say.

HARRY. Well, say it.

MUSH. It's the fly shams I'm talking about. You have to keep watching them all the time.

HARRY. What fly shams?

MUSH. Them smiling shams that start doing you favours because they want something off you. And if they don't do something for you, it's because they want something for that too.

HARRY. Person'lly, why should a man do nothing for nothing?

MUSH. I know, but they deny that, and you don't know where you are. Them fellas in charge say they're running things for what they can put into things. And they're just there for what they –

HARRY. Can get out of things.

MUSH. That's what has the world daft the way it is.

HARRY. I don't mind.

MUSH. Neither do I. But that's my opinion. And it's how they put on the serious faces that gets me most of all. Killed out, making big serious faces, organizing and that. But one little eye is doing a cute slow waltz all the time to see if the big boss, or the priest, or someone sees how killed out they are making faces.

HARRY. The holy ones is the worst.

MUSH. The ones that say 'Fawther' – like that: 'Fawther' – to the priest. And their sons is always thick. But they get the good job-stakes all the same. County Council and that.

HARRY. Them are the ones that gam on not to know you when they meet you.

MUSH. Even the ones was in your own class.

MICHAEL. That's because of the way they think you feel towards them. It's not how they feel. They don't mean –

HARRY. Thinking so hard when they meet you that they don't see you 'cause they're thinking so deep.

MUSH. Aw, but we're all equal and love your brother. Pray for them that persecute –

HARRY. An' calumniate –

MUSH. And fornicate you. (*They laugh.*)
(*To* Michael). Are you wise to them clients at all?

MICHAEL. I –

HARRY. He knows them.

MICHAEL. I know them. But they don't eat me.

MUSH. Did you ever notice the way they wrinkle up their noses, 'specially when –

MICHAEL. There's no need to –

HARRY. What?

MICHAEL. Exaggerate.

HARRY. He's not. They do. Exaggerating what anyway? You don't know what he was going to say, so how do you know it's exaggerating? See? Your big mistake is thinking they don't do it to you. Go on, Mush. They wrinkle up their noses.

MUSH. Yeh know, when they have on their four minx furs, and their crocodile skins shoes, they wrinkle up their noses.

HARRY. That's right.

MICHAEL. That's because of the smell of the furs and crocodiles.

HARRY (*rejects joke*). Naw-naw-naw-naw. The British boys! And smiles, looking sideways, and spitting over their left shoulders unknown.

MICHAEL. And Paddies.

HARRY. You're not a Paddy?

MICHAEL. We're all Paddies and the British boys know it.

HARRY. So we can't disappoint them if that's what they think. Person'lly, I wouldn't disappoint them.

MICHAEL. You won't fit into a place that way.

HARRY. Who wants to?

MICHAEL. I do.

HARRY. You want to be a British Paddy?

MICHAEL. No. But a lot of it is up to a man himself to fit into a place. Otherwise he might as well stay at home.

HARRY. It's up to a man himself?

MUSH. It's up to us?

MICHAEL. Give and take.

MUSH. Us? We've no chance. Har? Too much back-handin', too much palm-oil, too many Holy Marys pulling strings, and talking about merit.

HARRY. Too many people smiling. Too many –

MUSH. That's what I was saying.

HARRY. Too many people saying hello. Too many –

MUSH. That's what I was saying, Har.

HARRY. Hah?

MUSH. That everyone has a motive these days, even for a smile.

HARRY. Hah?

MUSH. That's what I was saying a minute ago.

HARRY (*considers for a moment*). Okay. What's your motive for going 'round with me?

MUSH. Hah? . . . Oh, it's . . . Well, we were in the same class. Remember? Me, you and Hugo in the back seat.

HARRY. But what are you smiling for? What do you want?

MUSH. Aw, jay, sham, don't take it too serious.

HARRY. Aw, but I do.

MUSH. But it's only with some people, Har, that –

HARRY. Yeh. What's Michael's motive?

MUSH. For what?

HARRY. For anything. For keeping us here.

MUSH. God, I don't know. Brothers, ye're all brothers.

HARRY. Naw – naw. Why do you do it, Mikey? And, I think, it's you following us. And you don't like us, I think. Hah? Tell us, Mush.

MUSH. God, I don't know. I suppose he has no choice.

HARRY. Hah? (*Then he laughs.*)

MUSH. Aw jay, I didn't mean it like that.

MICHAEL. We have enough bull talk around here.

MUSH. Well, I'm just going.

HARRY. Sit down.

MUSH. No, honest, the quare one should be waiting this hour. I just want to tell her I'm not available tonight. See you later. The best! Taw! (*Exits.*)

Pause. HARRY first, then MICHAEL, take out cigarettes and each lights one.

MICHAEL. Harry, I wanted to – We should have a talk.

HARRY. In case you think I'm drunk or something –

MICHAEL. No, I wasn't thinking that. I know you're not.

HARRY. What do you want to talk about?

MICHAEL. Well –

HARRY. Dada, is it?

MICHAEL. No, about Des.

HARRY. What about him?

MICHAEL. He's okay?

HARRY. He's okay.

MICHAEL. Well, he's the youngest.

HARRY. Yeh?

MICHAEL. He's only a kid and, well, he couldn't have much sense
yet.

HARRY. He won't be long wising-up over here – What are you
getting at?

MICHAEL. Well, it's up to the two of us – it's up to us to see he
goes home in, say, a week's time.

HARRY. An' why?

MICHAEL. Just, it's up to the two of us. He's only a kid and, well,
there's no one left at home now with Mama.

HARRY. Isn't there Dada?

MICHAEL. Des hasn't a chance over here.

HARRY. Chance of what?

MICHAEL. Look at it this way. It'd be sort of all right, wouldn't
it, if Des was something? Something in the family.

HARRY. Oh yeh, yeh, sure.

MICHAEL. We could be proud of him. Some one of us at last to
get something decent, a good job. Everyone has a boast about

something. We never had –

HARRY. There's Dada, an' –

MICHAEL. Des is still young. He could still get – *something*. We're all – all of us – well, straight talking, we don't count.

HARRY. A doctor maybe?

MICHAEL. Something – No – something.

HARRY. A solicitor maybe?

MICHAEL. No, just something, respectable, to be at home.

HARRY. Crap! Be something like you, is it, afraid of his shadow?

MICHAEL. Wait a minute –

BETTY *is standing in kitchen doorway.*

HARRY. Then we'd be proud of him, is it? It's up to the two of us, you and me. Crap, daff, bullshit! Do you think I'm an eejit? Des can do what he likes. Anyway he's staying on. We need him.

MICHAEL. I don't mean he has to be a doctor or a – What do you mean you need him?

HARRY. Just we need him, that's all. Anyway, he's staying. There's no one forcing him, but he's not going home yet.

BETTY. The Mulryans.

HARRY. Aaaa, Betty Batter bought a pound of butter! Sly lickle Betty does be earwiggin' at keyholes.

MICHAEL. For God's sake, you're not going to meet the Mulryans?

BETTY. Behind the old factory, up Rock's Lane.

HARRY. There was an old woman called Betty. You know that one? Mush told me. He knows all them ones.

MICHAEL. Hold on a minute now –

HARRY. There was an old woman called Betty, she slipped off the back of the sette; the sette it broke –

MICHAEL. But why?

HARRY. Why not?

MICHAEL. Why fight the Mulryans?

HARRY. Oh, a lot think, you know, we aren't able for them. But that wouldn't bother you. Just like Dada said, you've no pride.

MICHAEL. Dada is in on this already?

HARRY. We told him. The Mulryans was doing a lot of braggin' about what they'd do to us, so we sent them word we was claimin' them. Carneys versus Mulryans. All the Carneys: me, Iggy, Dada, Hugo and Des. Des'll be good. Five of us, seven of them.

MICHAEL. You're crazy. Do you know what you're doing this time? You know the kind they are, how they fight.

HARRY. You know how I fight. We're all iron men. Not just Iggy. Ask Dada. Fight all night, Michael. Anyone. (*Holds up his fist.*) Iron, look. Aw, but look, more iron. (*Withdraws from his pocket an ass-shoe which he wears as a knuckle duster. He gives* MICHAEL *a tap on the shoulder with it.*) A souvenir from Ireland. Iron, man. Let no one say there was ever a jibber in our family! Or was there? Hah? Not even one? Was there a jibber in our family, Michael? Go on, tell the missus.

MICHAEL. If you have to fight and get killed, don't draw Des into it, that's all.

HARRY. Jibber, jibber, what about the jibber?

MICHAEL. That sort of thing doesn't bother me at all.

HARRY. Hah?

BETTY. And you'd want to start looking for new digs.

HARRY. Hah?

MICHAEL. Just don't draw Des into it.

HARRY. Hah?

BETTY. We're going to do the place up.

HARRY. Now, Bitchey, how would you like to keep your English mouth out of it, and let the *man* of the house talk? (*To* MICHAEL.) What were you saying? You're tired of us, is it?

Mush says you've no choice. What do you think?

MICHAEL. My concern at the moment is for Des.

BETTY. You'll just have to get out, that's all.

HARRY. Look, why don't you go back to the skivvying in there? (*Men's voices off.*)

BETTY. You don't talk to me like that.

MICHAEL. Take it easy.

HARRY. You want to talk about Des? Well, I think we should have a talk too, about something else. That night with the Muslims.

MICHAEL. Another time. They're here.

HARRY. Two days in hospital.

MICHAEL *opens hall door.* IGGY, HUGO, DADA *and* DES *are coming in front door. They come into the living room.* DADA *is a fine tall man and aware of it. He is about sixty.* DES *is a big loose-limbed youth. Very eager to be accepted. At times given to cockiness. At the moment he behaves shyly. His face carries some mark of the fight.*

HARRY. We were just talking about ye.

DADA. Hah-ha, yes. How are you, Michael? (*Warm handshake for* MICHAEL.)

MICHAEL. You're welcome, ye're welcome. Come in. Don't say this is Des?

DES (*shyly; mutters*). Michael. (*Clumsy handshake.*)

DADA. That's Desmond.

MICHAEL. I thought you'd be a little lad that size. Come in.

DADA. Thank you.

MICHAEL. Sit down, sit down.

DADA. Thank you.

MICHAEL. Oh, this is my wife, Betty. Betty, this is Dada. And Des.

DADA (*rises, bows, shakes her hand warmly*). I've heard a lot about you. How do you do, ma'am!

BETTY (*impressed by him*). Mister Carney. (*She shakes hands with* DES, *who remains seated.*) How do you do! Let me take your coats.

MICHAEL. Yes, take off your coats.

DADA. I hope we aren't too much trouble, inconvenience.

BETTY. Not at all, not at all.

MICHAEL. Not at all.

BETTY *takes coats out to hall.*

DADA. Well, you're looking well, Michael. That's a nice woman you got.

MICHAEL. You're looking well yourself.

DADA. Can't help it, can't help it.

MICHAEL. No, I suppose . . . How's Mama? (*Slight pause.* DADA *feels there is an accusation in such questions.*)

DADA. . . . Fine, fine. Sent her love. To you all. I wanted her to come over with Desmond and I'd stay at home – Didn't I, Desmond? – Or even come with the two of us, yes, but you know your mother. Somebody might run away with the house. And – Hah-haa!

MICHAEL. . . . Was it rough crossing?

DADA. A bit, a bit. (*Chuckles.*) Desmond didn't feel too good. It didn't affect an old sailor like me though.

MICHAEL. No.

BETTY. Will I get the tea now?

MICHAEL. Oh yes, do, do.

DADA (*rising*). Don't go to any trouble now, ma'am. Just a cup.

BETTY (*exiting to kitchen*). It's no trouble at all, Mr Carney.

DADA. Yes, nice woman you got, Michael.

MICHAEL. I'd hardly know Des, honestly: he's got so big. How are things with you, Des?

DES. Good.

DADA. He has shoulders like the old man all right, hasn't he?

MICHAEL. It must be hard trying to keep a lad like that fed at home.

DADA (*slight pause*). . . . We want for nothing at home.

MICHAEL (*quickly*). I know, I know. Just coddin' about Des growing so much. (DADA *looks at* HARRY, IGGY *and* HUGO.) Oh, a thing I was often thinking about. Them trees we planted. Do you remember? Did they grow?

DES. Oh, yeh.

MICHAEL. Before I – before I came over here, Des and myself were down in the wood one day and we got these five young ash trees. And we planted them at the wall at the back of the house. Five of them, one for each of us, five sons, you know. I was wondering, did they all grow?

DES. They did. I think. Some of them.

DADA. I never seen them. It's dangerous anyway having trees near a house like that.

HUGO. Storms and all.

DADA. Not only that, but the carbon dioxide. Gas. The trees give it out at night. The carbon dioxide. Tid poison you. (*The sons, except* MICHAEL, *provide a good audience for this sort of thing from* DADA.)

MICHAEL. What are you at now?

DADA. Ah – Work, is it?

MICHAEL. Yeh.

DADA. Something lined up, you know.

MICHAEL. Yeh?

DADA. Yes. A good job on the way. (*Slight pause.*) Hah-haa! You never lost it, Michael. The old worrier. Isn't he the old worrier, lads? (*Inviting them to laugh with him.*) Isn't he the old worrier?

MICHAEL (*To* DES). What do you think of Coventry?

HUGO. Dother way round: what does Coventry think of him, eh, Dessie? (DES *feels the bruise on his face.*)

DADA. Yes, Coventry has made its impression already.

MICHAEL. Is it okay?

DES. Nothing. Two fellas in the – the, yeh know, of the pub. And they were laughing, yeh know, and talking about – well, Paddies.

HUGO. Wait'll you hear this. Go on, Des.

DES. Sort of jybin', well, sort of jybin' Iggy and Hugo. They must have been listening to us inside. And I sort of went across to them and I said, 'Well, I'm a Paddy', I said –

MICHAEL. You shouldn't have taken any notice of –

HARRY. } Go on, Des.
HUGO. } Shush!

DES. Well, they went for me. Well, I had to defend myself. Well, I had to try to. Two of them. One of them sort of came at me with his head, his forehead –
HUGO. The nut –

DES. And I got this. (*Bruise.*) And stars for a minute, and then, well, lights out. (*All except* MICHAEL *laugh.*)

DADA. I wish I was there when it happened. Paddies! Irish people talk better than English people do.

HUGO. And O'Connell Street is the widest street in – in the world.

DADA. But wait a minute, Desmond. You said, well I'm a Paddy, right?

DES. I said –

DADA. And where were you standing then?

DES. Well, I was – Well, I went across, and they were – you know? –

DADA. But you were standing in the middle of the – the – the toilet?

DES. They were sort of – You know? And –

DADA. And they went for you, right?

DES. Well, they were – ah – and I let go just when –

DADA. But you didn't connect proper?

DES. I –

DADA. Properly –

DES. They were coming for me, and I –

DADA. They tore into you. What did you do then?

DES. When they – ?

DADA. Yes, rushed you.

DES. I – they – well, his head –

DADA. You waited for them, right?

DES. I –

DADA. Wrong. Wrong, lad. Big mistake. You should have – Well, ask Ignatius, Henry. I bet they'd agree. You shouldn't have stood there.

HUGO. Called us.

DADA. No. I'm surprised at you, Hubert. Your back to the wall, man. Protection, the wall, your back to it. Ignatius?

IGGY. No one behind you.

DADA. Your back to the wall.

IGGY. And keep swingin'.

DADA. Remember that now. You won't always have me or your brothers. So what do you do?

DES. Get back to the wall – and keep swingin'.

DADA. And a last piece of advice. Don't ever go expecting anyone, a friend or anyone, to help you in a fight. While you're looking around for that friend, you could be finished. If someone joins in, okay, but you keep your eyes on your man.

HARRY. And if someone joins in, you don't run.

DES. But I wouldn't.

DADA. There's good stuff in Desmond.

DES. I wouldn't.

DADA. No fear of him doing that.

HARRY (*looks at* MICHAEL). Just in case he might be another four-minute sham.

DES. I know a thing or two.

HARRY. I know. (*Looks at* MICHAEL.) We've a sort of joke here about sprinters.

MICHAEL (*exiting to kitchen*). Is the tea ready? (DADA *winks at* MICHAEL's *back for the quiet amusement of the others.*)

HARRY. Did you not see the bottle? (DES *looks at him.*) . . . On the little windowsill. Dust and cobwebs on it. Did you not see it? What was that doing there?

IGGY. Hard hittin's enough.

HARRY. Naw-naw, a bottle is better than a fist. A broken bottle is better than two fists. See the fear of God it puts into them and they start backin' away from you.

IGGY. I seen fellas fightin' better because of the fear of God.

HARRY. Naw, not with the spikey glass in front of their eyes. They don't know what to do they're so frightened. And he tries to save himself with his hands, and they get bleeding first –

MICHAEL (*entering with some tea things*). Take it easy, Harry –

HARRY. You pay attention, Des –

MICHAEL. Take it easy –

HARRY. Michael, our miler, don't like glass, he don't like blood, he don't like us, he don't like anything!

IGGY. W-w-what if you've no bottle, what then?

HARRY. Always this. (*Produces the ass-shoe.*)

HUGO. Or a chain or a rasp or a belt or a chair.

HARRY. You pay attention, Des. You be my 'prentice and I'll make you a tradesman, a good 'un.

MICHAEL. Come on, the tea is getting cold.

HARRY. Which is best you think, Dada, bottles or just fists? Is Iggy or me right?

MICHAEL. Dada, stow it. This kind of talk is –

DADA. Aw, this is a good healthy argument. It could save a man's life. Now, fists or bottles. Well, when I was your age I could flatten any man that came my way with my fists. Hah-haa, Ignatius! And I still can, make no mistake about that. One man, two men or three men. After that – Hah-haa, Harry! – I see no harm in taking up a – a club to even up the numbers. Do you get me now?

HARRY. Why take the risk ever, fighting fair with anyone?

DADA. It's up to yourself. Can you take him without a club?

HARRY. Why ask the question at all?

DADA. Yes.

HARRY. Hah? A fight's a fight, Dada.

HUGO. That's right.

HARRY. Hah?

DADA. That's right. It's a very personal question, and up to the man involved.

BETTY (*entering with tea things*). Would you like to sit at the table now?

DADA. Thank you, ma'am.

HARRY. Hah?

DADA. Ah, the tea! (DADA *and* DES *start to eat.*)

BETTY. Tea, Harry? (HARRY *ignores her.*)

DADA. Very tasty. You're a very good cook, ma'am.

BETTY. Oh, I would like to have done something nicer for you, Mr Carney.

DADA. Very tasty. (BETTY *exits to the kitchen*.) Yes, very nice woman you got there, Michael.

MUSH (*enters*). God bless the work! Is Harry here? (*Sees* HARRY.) One of your long-haired ones is waiting up the road.

DADA. Are you courting, Henry?

The others laugh. HARRY *scowls.*

MUSH (*to* DADA). I hear things are very bad in Mary Horan's country, Mr Carney?

DADA. What?

MICHAEL. Ireland: Mary Horan's country.

MUSH. The economy destroyed since the demand for St. Patrick's day badges fell. (*They laugh. To* HARRY.) Bhuil tú ag teacht? (HARRY *exits, followed by* MUSH. *As he goes out.*) Slán libh!

DADA. Slán leat!

BETTY (*entering from kitchen with a bowl of fruit*). I've just put on some more food, Mr Carney, it won't take long.

HUGO. Can you talk Irish, Dada?

DADA. I'm fluent at it. Many's the conversation I have at home with John Quinlan. You know, John, the doctor. And Anthony Heneghan – he's an architect. At the club. And often, for the sport of it, we talk nothing but Irish all night. At the club.

MICHAEL. I think I knew Anthony Heneghan.

DADA. A grand young man, scholarly, fond of his jar.

MICHAEL. He was a few years ahead of me at school.

DADA. You should have gone on for an architect.

MICHAEL. Two years in a secondary school wouldn't have made an architect out of me.

DADA. Your aunt would have kept you on at that school, but instead you kept running back to us every chance you got. I didn't think you were that fond of us in them days. Hah, lads? (*Smiles at the others.*) But it's a grand job though, an architect, and plenty of cash in it. And nothing to it. Even Anthony admits that. Sure, anyone can draw a house.

MICHAEL (*to* DES). How long do ye think ye'll stay?

DADA. I'll take a week, maybe ten days, to see ye're all okay.

MICHAEL (*to* DES). Yeh?

DES. I think I'll stay another while. I'll get something here to keep me going. Harry said he'd fix me up anyway.

MICHAEL. I thought you were getting into the new factory at home?

DES. A lousy few quid. I don't fancy it much.

DADA. The lad has the wandering bug too. Do you think you'd like it here, Desmond?

MICHAEL. It'd be better for you at home.

DADA. I thought you two used to get on well.

DES. I think I'll try it for a while, Michael.

DADA. Now you want to send him back, and he's just over.

MICHAEL. Wouldn't it be all right for you to have someone at home?

DADA. I didn't think I looked that old. Do I, boys?

MICHAEL. Well, for Mama then.

DADA. Naturally we want to keep the boy, but I wouldn't keep a lad from what he wants himself, just for walking around the house. Amn't I right? That was always my way. Free will.

DES. There's too many bosses in that factory job. Slave-drivers. You don't have to lick no one's shoes over here.

MICHAEL. No one would like it better than me for you to be over here, but the job at home is sound, secure.

DADA. Why are you putting him off?

MICHAEL. There isn't a lot over here for anyone, Dada. At home is a better bet.

DADA. You're casting a reflection on your brothers, Michael.

MICHAEL. He could go to the Tech and all at night, Dada. Don't you agree? And then, maybe later –

DADA. The trouble with you, Michael, is you've no pride. I don't want people, twopence-half-penny guys, ordering a son of mine, a Carney, to clean up after them.

MICHAEL. I'm not going again' you now, Dada, but what do you think he'll be doing over here?

DADA. I'm not a man that believes in apron-strings. Desmond is the youngest, but he's no child. I let the rest of you make your own choices, decisions. Free will. Always believed in that. So, if you failed, you can't blame me. They were your own decisions. Oh, but you didn't fail, and I'm proud, and you did it on your own. No matter who is casting suspicious reflections. I was always a proud man, everyone will tell you that. I have my pride, I know, but, as I said, a man must have pride. And, in the words of the great Gene Tunney, a man must fight back. His father was a Mayoman too.

MICHAEL (*to* IGGY). What do you think, should he stay or go?

IGGY. Not my affair.

MICHAEL. A straight answer.

HUGO. We need him.

MICHAEL (*to* IGGY). Does he know what for?

IGGY. Let her (*Des*) do the choosing. Like Dada said, she's no baby.

DES. I'd like to stay, Michael; honest.

MICHAEL. Don't be a fool. You don't know what's here for you.

HUGO. He isn't a fool.

DES. I'm needed. This is for the family.

DADA. Well said.

DES. It wouldn't be fair if I went back. The Mulryans. Seven of them. I don't think it'd be fair to back out. Anyway, I wouldn't.

DADA. No, it wouldn't be right. If the Mulryans is bragging about what they'd do to sons of mine, then they have to be learned different. Differently.

MICHAEL. And when is this great event to take place?

IGGY. Any time they like.

HUGO. We sent them word.

DADA. And I'm proud of ye, your ability, as my father was proud of me; afraid of no man, able for all.

MICHAEL. A fine man isn't a thug.

DADA. Any man can't fight isn't worth his salt. I'm restraining myself, Michael. A man must fight back at – at – at – A man must fight back. I'm a fighting man myself, and I can talk with the best, and mix with them. And as Anthony Heneghan said to me one evening –

MICHAEL. This is no place for another Carney.

DADA. What? . . . Aren't we not welcome here? I told ye, didn't I, he'd start it.

MICHAEL. I'm not starting anything. Dada, listen –

DADA. Don't tell me to listen! It wasn't easy for me to come here, but I came. That's me, forgive and forgot, all for the sake of the family. I came here in good faith, and the welcome I get is a barrage of insinuating questions.

MICHAEL. All I'm asking is a simple thing.

DADA. No!

MICHAEL. No one said anything about good faith.

DADA. Are you sneering at what I'm saying? At your father. Do ye see him, lads?

MICHAEL. Honest to God! All I'm saying is –

DADA. Do ye hear him?

MICHAEL. Should Des go home. I think it's better.

DADA. And whom is the rightful judge on that matter?

MICHAEL. God, that's exactly what you used to say to me fifteen years ago.

DADA. I'm not welcome, boys.

HUGO. By God, he won't throw no one out and me here.

MICHAEL. Who said anything about that? I just said –

DES. I can take care of myself, honest, Michael.

DADA. No, he knows better, Desmond.

MICHAEL. What am I?

DADA. What? What are you saying?

MICHAEL. What's Harry? (*Points to* IGGY *and* HUGO.) What are they? And what's he going to be? (*Des*) What are we, the Carneys?

DADA. Oh, I've my pride if you haven't. As I said –

MICHAEL } And what are –
DADA   } I'm afraid of no man alive and I can talk with the best
               and –
MICHAEL. What are you?

DADA. . . . There's no change in you. We're rotten – the lot of us – except you.

MICHAEL. It's not my fault.

DADA. And is it mine?

HUGO. Dada's first night over. No one should talk to their father like that.

DADA. No, Hubert, they shouldn't. But he's our educated boy. I thought we were rid of you years ago when I flung you out, but you keep sticking on.

HUGO. He that asked us to stay here.

DADA. He wants to live with men, and he hasn't a gut in his body. Worse, he wants to give the orders. You! You're like a mangy dog: the more it's kicked, the harder it sticks on. That's you! And he calls ye rotten. Him! It's a good job I came over. And you're saying Desmond is going home?

MICHAEL. No need to get excited.

DADA. Wha'? What!

MICHAEL. There's no one trying to give orders. I just want us all to get on. We're a family, and –

DADA. And who is disrupting the family?

MICHAEL. No need to get excited.

DADA. Don't try a bluff! You should know it won't work with me. You can talk a bit, but you can't act. Actions speak louder than words. The man of words fails the man of action. Or maybe you have changed, got brave? Maybe you'll act?

DES. I think you're both getting worked up about nothing.

DADA. You don't know him.

MICHAEL. Who do you think you are?

DADA. The same man I always was.

MICHAEL. This isn't twenty years ago.

DADA (*takes off his belt*). The same belt even. Look.

MICHAEL. Are you mad? This is my house you're in now, remember.

DADA. Aw, aren't you great to have a house, doing well. We're proud of you. Is it paid for though? It doesn't change things whose house it is. Or maybe you are the boss here, what? Instead of your faithful dog look. Any more instructions, doggie, any more sneering?

BETTY *is entering with tray of food.*

MICHAEL. We're all grown up. We're not kids now.

DADA. *We're? We're?* I'm talking to you! You, on your own! Are you grown up over us?

MICHAEL. You can't walk in here and –

DADA *sees* BETTY: *he hesitates for a moment – embarrassed – then he lashes the table with his belt savagely; he feels he has let himself down; it drives him to excesses.*

DADA. Up, muck and trash, we'll put him to bed like in the old days!

IGGY *and* HUGO *stand, one each side of* DADA. *The whole attitude is threatening.* MICHAEL *shakes his hands, meaning calm down, and exits hall door.* BETTY *follows.* DADA *hesitates, then laughs harshly after* BETTY.

Hah-haaaa! . . . I showed him. He never changed a bit. Like old times! (*He throws his arms around* HUGO *and* IGGY.) But do ye know I was very lonely for ye at home. I'm glad I came. I'm glad. Yes. Aa, ye're great lads. (DES, *seated, is looking up at them.*)

Act Two

The following night.

DADA *is viewing himself from different angles in the mirror. But eventually he is standing motionless, his face hopeless, looking at himself in the mirror.* MICHAEL *is heard coming down the stairs.* DADA *reacts indecisively. Eventually, a moment of childish defiance when he takes out a cigar and considers lighting it. He changes his mind and puts it back in his pocket.* MICHAEL *enters. He wants to speak to* DADA. *He adjusts his tie unnecessarily, recombs his hair, finds a handkerchief in the sideboard. The silence goes on, though it is obvious that both of them would like to talk. Eventually,* DADA *exits, whistling tunelessly.* MICHAEL *is annoyed that the opportunity for a private talk has passed. Then* DADA *re-enters, and starts with a blurt.*

DADA. For the sake of the family – ah – Wish to – to – to. Friction a bad thing domestically, a bad thing. . . . Yes. (MICHAEL *is delighted. He doesn't know how to begin. He opens his mouth to speak.*) No. Sufficient said. Yes. Internal friction always bad domestically. Yes.

MICHAEL. . . . Will you smoke, Dada?

DADA. No, I'll smoke – (*His hand to his pocket for cigar. He changes his mind.*) Ah – I will. Thank you. (MICHAEL *lights cigarettes.*) Thank you. (*Pause.*) Very nice cigarette. (*Pause.*)

DADA.   } I hope –
MICHAEL. } I wanted to –

DADA. Yes?

MICHAEL. No, Dada, what were you going to say?

DADA. Oh, just, I – I hope you appreciate the moral courage it took for me to – Duty.

MICHAEL. Yes, I do.

DADA. It wasn't easy for me to – Internal friction bad – and

MICHAEL. Yes, I know, I appreciate it.

DADA. Duty.

MICHAEL. Yes.

DADA. Family.

MICHAEL. Yes. That's what I wanted to talk about too.

DADA (*wary*). Well, maybe we should postpone – What?

MICHAEL. It's a good few years – It's a long time since we saw you, and – Well, we weren't home for a long time.

DADA. Yes?

MICHAEL. We're changed more than you know.

DADA. Do you think so, son?

MICHAEL. You haven't – I mean, the others. They've gone completely –

DADA. Spirited.

MICHAEL. No. They're big names.

DADA. Big names?

MICHAEL. No, I don't mean in that sense.

DADA. Carneys.

MICHAEL. I mean, around this area. And I was getting a bit worried, and I moved out here too. You know?

DADA. Henry is talking about buying a car.

MICHAEL. I thought I could sober them up.

DADA. A lot of prestige attached to a car.

MICHAEL. Straight talking, Dada. Harry has a couple of women working for him. You know, you know what I mean. He even suggested I give him the front room for his – business. And Iggy is foreman of a heavy-digging job just outside town, and under Harry's supervision he sacks and hires Harry's clients, mostly darkies and men that find it hard to get work. And then, every pay-day, they collect a pound or two apiece off all that Iggy hired.

DADA. They're in it in a big way?

MICHAEL. No. It's not that big. They're trying to be fly, they think they're being fly. There's no one to tell them.

DADA. They could be big.

MICHAEL. No. It's where it's all leading to.

DADA. You wouldn't turn down a soft pound.

MICHAEL. I know, I know. I'm as light-fingered as anyone. But it's a can of paint, a bit of timber, a few bricks –

DADA. Make your money fast. It's the only way. That's the way they all did it. Then buy a business. The whole family could be in on it. Michael Carney and Sons. Hah-haa, Michael Carney *Senior* & Sons.

MICHAEL. Sure, I know, it'd be great, but –

DADA. What?

MICHAEL. Well, the police –

DADA (*snaps*). What about them? I know about the police. I was one myself.

MICHAEL. But it's where it's all leading to. And I've this awful feeling that something terrible is going to happen.

DADA. No danger. I'm very fast to size up a good thing, opportunity. Cute Henry never said a word about his enterprises.

MICHAEL. Do you know what it is –

DADA. Michael G. Carney & Sons, over a shop, Michael. There's plenty of time later for respectability when we've showed them.

MICHAEL. Do you know what I mean when I say he has a few little girls working for him? Kids. I see them down the road in the little café. Don't you know what it is to take a couple of quid off a workingman every week?

DADA. Make – the – most – of – opportunity.

MICHAEL. No. No! And you know this is terrible the same as I do.

DADA. They're the only ones at it, are they?

MICHAEL. No, but –

DADA. Well, then –

MICHAEL. No.

DADA (*viciously*). And – what – do – you – think – I – should – do?

MICHAEL. Well, the first thing –

DADA. Drag Desmond home behind me?

MICHAEL (*pauses, considering this*). . . . It's just I have this awful feeling. Well, maybe I shouldn't have brought that up last night. Just as you said, he's no child now. And he's bright enough. And let him have a look around for a while, and then decide for himself.

DADA. So I'm not the fool you think I am?

MICHAEL. I never thought that. The first thing is this fight with the Mulryans.

DADA. Don't fight?

MICHAEL. You know yourself what can happen.

DADA. I don't know.

MICHAEL. You wouldn't be doing it for me, Dada.

DADA. Oh-ho-no, I wouldn't be doing it for you. I never did anything for you, did I?

MICHAEL. No, I don't mean that. You're the only one they'll listen to.

DADA. I know.

MICHAEL. Well, look, do you honestly – A straight question now – Do you honestly think they should fight?

DADA. Enough said. You're always right, I'm always wrong, the defaulter. No, say no more. My advice and views –

MICHAEL. Stay a minute –

DADA. Are respected, sought by the best everywhere, anywhere I go. But you know it all.

MICHAEL. Well, what are you going to do about it?

DADA. I've no more time for you. I know how you think. I came in here like a man to – to – to – And this is the reception. (*Takes out his cigar and holds it up defiantly.*)

MICHAEL. Well, what are you going to do?

DADA. Enough said. My responsibility, boy, my responsibility. (*Exits up stairs.*)

BETTY *and* DES *enter.*

BETTY (*throwing herself into a chair*). Phew! It's warm outside. Des and I were going to go off somewhere for the night, Michael. Weren't we?

DES (*laughs*). Yeh.

BETTY. What do you think of that, Michael?

MICHAEL (*absently*). Yeh.

BETTY (*to* DES). Wouldn't you like to be as handsome as your brother?

DES (*laughs*). Yeh.

MICHAEL (*irritably*). Then you could get a pretty little woman like me: English.

BETTY. We must get a nice girl for you, Des. I know! That pretty girl in the paper shop on the corner. Yes, I think she would be –

MICHAEL (*angrily*). Why are you always trying to organize other people? Do you think they don't know how to organize their own lives? What business is it of yours? (*Realizes he is being unfair; he tries to pass it off.*) Des is in no hurry with the birds, are you? Don't be in any hurry to go to the altar. See what happened to me.

DES. About fifteen years' time.

BETTY. Oh no, you'll be too old then, you'll be past it, like your brother. (DES *laughs.*) But when you do get married, make sure –

MICHAEL. You don't see your mother-in-law too often. Mum and Dad. Make sure –

BETTY. There's worse than mother-in-laws you can see too often.

MICHAEL. What?

BETTY. I said there's worse than mother-in-laws to have around.

DES. Wives.

MICHAEL (*laughs*). Good boy, Dessie.

BETTY. That's very funny, I'm sure.

MICHAEL. Oh-ho, she's getting narked.

BETTY. No, I'm not. It would take more than that – not like some. My advice to you is don't get married at all. Honestly, Irishmen shouldn't. (*Exits and goes upstairs.*)

MICHAEL. By gum, lad, hah?

DES. Is she crabbed? (*Upset.*)

MICHAEL. No. (*Sighs; then.*) . . . I just seem to be thinking a bit different from other people these days.

DES. Dada? We saw him going up the stairs when we came in.

MICHAEL. Talk about a man!

DES. Ary, he's all right. He's contrary at times, and, often, he isn't so practical. But it's always the way with clever men. (MICHAEL *looks at him but lets him talk on.*) You know how it is. And he finds it hard to talk about little things. And a strange thing, about a month ago, he stole an overcoat. . . . Yes! Dada.

MICHAEL. He never did anything like that before.

DES. I know. And he stole it out of that golf club, where he likes to drink. And it was that Anthony Heneghan's coat. And he just threw it over a wall coming home. I don't know why. He didn't want the coat.

MICHAEL. And did anything happen?

DES. No. But he can't drink there anymore. He doesn't know we heard about it, Mama and I. (*Pause.*)

MICHAEL. How is she?

DES. Oh, she's – she's fine.

MICHAEL. How are you fixed for dust?

DES. I'm okay.

MICHAEL. Here's a few quid anyway. You might want something.

DES. No, I'm okay, honest.

MICHAEL (*pushes money into* DES's *top pocket*). Here, take it, don't be silly. If you're stuck later let me know. You might want to get something for Mama.

DES. Thanks.

MICHAEL. She's all right, is she?

DES. Yeh. Fine. She said to tell you come home for Christmas.

MICHAEL. I might.

DES. No, she said to be sure you come. To tell you.

MICHAEL. I might all right.

DES. She said even for a few days.

MICHAEL. It's over ten years, yeh know.

DES. God, it'd be great. Wouldn't it be great if we were all at home together at Christmas? Walking up town, us all together. I think she gets sort of lonely. Us all gone, you know.

MICHAEL. Yeh.

DES. I think she gets sort of lonely.

MICHAEL (*getting irritable*). Yes. He never made things easy for her. He – (*Restrains himself.*)

DES. Well, he got a fair amount of tough luck, like. But you'd manage a few days anyway, and try and pull with himself. He can be understanding too.

MICHAEL (*reflectively*). Yeh. I never thought he was stupid. If he was I wouldn't mind. Just getting dafter. Not stupid. Just hare-brained.

HARRY *and* MUSH *enter.*

HARRY. Who's hare-brains? You it must be, Mush, they're talking about.

MUSH. Not me, I'm a rabbit man myself. Remember the rabbit, Har? God made the bees and –

HARRY. The bees made honey;

MUSH. God made man and –

HARRY. Man made money –

MUSH. God made the rabbit to run around the grass –

HARRY. }
MUSH. } God made the greyhound to catch him by the arse.

HARRY. I hear that Dada is a bit of a greyhound too, though, hah? I hear he can still make you run.

MICHAEL. How're the Flanagans, Des?

DES. The ones used to live next door?

MICHAEL. Used?

DES. They moved into a new house a few years ago. (MICHAEL *nods to* HARRY.)

HARRY (*copies the nod*). What's that supposed to mean?

MICHAEL. They've a new house.

HARRY. Yeh?

MUSH (*laughs*). Pookey Flanagan. That's what we used call him. He used sweep the roads.

MICHAEL. That's right. He was a road-sweeper. And one of his sons became an engineer, and there was a girl that became a nun, and another of them was at the university when I left. All from the dirt of the roads.

HARRY. Yeh, that's very interesting.

MICHAEL. But you were saying yesterday, as far as I remember, that people like us haven't a chance to get on.

HARRY. I didn't say that *I'm* not getting by, did I, in my own special little person'l way, did I?

MICHAEL. And what was Dada?

DES. A policeman once.

MICHAEL. Yeh.

HARRY. Yeh what?

MICHAEL. And what's that old saying of yours, Mush: 'Why wouldn't he get on, a policeman's son?' We're a policeman's sons.

HARRY. Dada did all right as far as I'm concerned.

MICHAEL. Roaring around the town, louder than someone shouting the water is to be turned off, that the Carneys are the best men?

MUSH. Times were hard, Michael, in them days.

MICHAEL. Harder for Pookey Flanagan.

HARRY. Why you trying to knock him? You think he belted you too much? Person'lly I don't think you ever got belted enough.

MICHAEL. I'd just like some people to know that a lot of the rubbish talked isn't the gospel.

HARRY (*looks at* DES). Hah?

DES. I hear about the old days even yet.

MICHAEL. They're hard to live down.

DES. No, a lot of people at home talk about Iggy – and ye all – with a sort of respect. They do, Michael. And they know Iggy is called the Iron Man over here. Even outside the town, they're, well – kind of afraid of the name Carney.

MICHAEL. Afraid?

HARRY. Afraid.

MUSH. I'd agree with that.

DES. They sort of look up to it.

MICHAEL. Come off it. Who looks up to us? I'll tell you – I could tell you a million things.

HARRY. Yeh, you're clever.

MICHAEL. I was up town one day with another fella, and we were passing Doonan's. You know, Doonan, the postman. And his kids were playing outside. And one of them hit the other with a stone, just as we were passing. And Doonan came out. He didn't ask who did it or anything, but when he saw me he shouted, 'Go home, you tinker! Go back to your tent, Carney!' He never asked the kids, he never looked at the fella with me. I was the tinker.

HARRY. Yeh? An' what did you do?

MICHAEL. Well, I didn't think there was any point in saying anything to a man like –

HARRY. What would you do, Des?

DES. I'd have split him wide open, I would! Give him cause to call names.

MICHAEL. And then you have another incident chalked up for –

DES. But you didn't start it.

HARRY. That wouldn't worry *him*.

MICHAEL. But you were saying there was respect.

HARRY. You're a coward, that's all.

MICHAEL. But you were saying they look up to us. (*Looks at* MUSH.) *Hah? Hah*, Mush? Do *you, hah*, look up to us, *hah?*

MUSH. Hah? (*Short pause.*) . . . Hah-haa, Har! Remember McQuaide, the school-teacher? (*He starts to cavort about imitating the mannerisms of the school-teacher, and mimicking him.*) Come here to me, O'Reilly! Come out heere, you moron! Aa, look at heem! Look at the cut of heem, boys! Thy knees have seen water at Baptism last! Aa, he thinks it's funny heemself! (*Grabs his cheek between thumb and forefinger, slapping the other cheek with his free hand.*) Now – now – now! The eembecile finds heemself funny! Where's your learned friend? Mr Henry Carney, we'll have your catechism. Up – up – up, wheen I speak to you! Who made the world?

DES. MacAlpine! (*They laugh. Then* HARRY *takes a knife off the table and lifts locks of* MUSH's *hair with it.*)

HARRY. He ever do that to you?

MUSH (*a little frightened*). Yeh.

HARRY. To see if they was any lice, fleas, on you, hah?

MUSH. Yeh.

HARRY (*to* MICHAEL). But, I suppose, he never done it to you?

MICHAEL. Teachers have to –

HARRY. Why do they only have to do it to some? You'd imagine – They're teachers! – Polite! – Polite to do it to everyone. Any time I got pox or crabs, wasn't off the ones I thought I'd get it off. Lifting your hair like that. Holding his breath in your ear. Then munchin' them nuts, moving on to the next place in your head, and slobbery bits of white nuts slobbering outside his lips.

MUSH. And the oranges, Har.

HARRY. He was a pig!

MUSH. And the little pen-knife he had for peeling his apples.

HARRY. And asking you what you had for your dinner – Not because he cared. And person'l questions. (*Releases* MUSH. *To* MICHAEL.) He never asked you, I suppose?

MICHAEL. Yes.

HARRY. Yeh – yeh – yes. He asked all the class one day, 'What you going to be when you grow up?' Some said –

MUSH. Yeh! I said that day a lighthouse keeper. And he said –

HARRY. Some said engine drivers, and things. And Dada was then sort of selling things round the countryside. Suits and coats and ties and things. Well, just when he came to my turn, and I was ready to say what I was going to be, he said first, 'I suppose, Carney, you'll be a Jewman.' (*pedlar*)

DES. What were you going to say anyway you'd be?

HARRY (*sincerely*). Priest. (*Then he looks defiantly at them*). . . . I said it too, after he saying the other thing, and he laughed.

MUSH. The friggin' bastard.

HARRY. Yeh. The friggin' pig. And all the other friggin' pigs.

(*Suddenly, to* MICHAEL). You'd still salute McQuaide?

MICHAEL. I haven't lost any sleep over him for years. Would *you* still salute him?

HARRY (MICHAEL *has found a mark*). Aw, Jesus, you're very clever! No – no – naaw, I wouldn't! I fight!

MICHAEL. And what good is that? Be called an Iron Man?

HARRY. No!

MICHAEL. Why so?

HARRY. Ary why – why – why! – Why my arse – Why anything?

MICHAEL. But you've no reason, see.

HARRY. But, see, I have! I have reasons, see, all right! I'll fight anyone that wants to, that don't want to! I'm not afraid of nobody! They don't just ignore me! They don't ask me what I had for my dinner! They don't –

DES. They? Who?

HARRY. Oh, they – they – they – they – THEM! Them shams! You all know who I'm talking about. You know them. You know them. He knows them. (*To* MICHAEL.) You suck up to them, I fight them. Who do they think most of, me or you?

MICHAEL. If it comes to that –

HARRY. Aw, do they now? They think more of you? I can make them afraid. What can you do? They notice me, do they notice you? They don't pretend to notice me, *but they do.* And they're beginning to notice me more and more. And they know clean and straight where I stand. And I know where I stand. And I like it. And I'm pleased. Person'lly, I'm very pleased. (*Exits to kitchen.*)

MICHAEL. I'm going up to a club up the road. Do you want to come? I won't be long.

DES. I've to give Dada a shout. We're all going out.

MICHAEL *exits. As he goes out,* IGGY *and* HUGO *are coming in the front door.*

HUGO (*in the hall*). Well, Killer! (IGGY *and* HUGO *come into the room.*) Heigh-up! Where's the preacher off to all spruced up?

MUSH. Up to Father Rowan's place. I'd better be off myself.

HUGO (*laughs. To* IGGY). That's the place they put you out of one night, and you broke the billiard table first.

IGGY (*in agreement, 'Aw'*). Aw. Snakes 'n' ladders place.

HARRY (*off, in kitchen*). Where you off to, Mush?

MUSH. Ye're all dolled-up beside me, Har. Down to get a clean under-pants: you'd never know who'd you'd meet on a Saturday night.

HARRY. See you in The Bower later.

MUSH. Right. Taw! The best! (*Exits.*)

HARRY (*enters eating a sandwich. To* DES). You didn't go off with Michael? (*And doesn't wait for a reply; to* IGGY.) Ye go to the pictures?

IGGY. Aw.

HUGO. Them singing shams is all played out. All mouths and firing roses at women. (*Has been trying to make the television work.*) You'd think he'd get this fixed again. This is a very bad stable we're in. (*Sees* HARRY *eating. Goes out to the kitchen.*)

IGGY. D'ye remember that kiddie, Hopalong Cassidy? You never see her now.

HUGO (*off, in kitchen*). He was a tough-un.

IGGY. (I) Used like her.

HUGO (*off*). I never seen him in a bad picture. Did ye ever notice he used never bother with the women? I never seen him kiss a jane once.

HARRY. I did. Just once though. Yeh see, in this picture, this one was after getting shot, and she was dying, out on the prairie, and Hoppy come along, singing or laughing at something, or admiring the view for himself. On his horse. And she was dying. So he seen her, and he jumped down. And she said, 'Hoppy, kiss me, I'm dying', or something.

HUGO (*entering, eating a sandwich*). Hah?

HARRY. 'Hoppy, kiss me, I'm dying' – Something.

HUGO. And did he?

HARRY. He did.

HUGO. Well, I suppose he couldn't help it.

IGGY. I seen that one! And Hoppy – Well, she nearly started crying, and grinding her teeth, like that. Aw yes, she was the kiddie. Used like her.

HUGO. Where's Dada?

DES. I'd better give him a shout. I don't think he's so flush with the money.

HUGO. We sent him nothing for a few weeks.

They start a 'whip round' – HARRY, IGGY and HUGO contributing a few pounds each. DES is going to call DADA. He opens the door, and DADA is found standing outside, in the hall.

DES. Oh, I was just –

DADA (*ignores DES. Enters*). Boys, nothing like forty winks in the evening. (*Sees money on the table.*) Oh? Has someone too much money?

HARRY. That's yours.

IGGY. You must have left it there.

HUGO. We all chipped in.

HARRY exits to the kitchen.

DADA. Boys, it's hard not to say a few words at times like this. I know it's not necessary – I am sure of that – nevertheless, permit me. And, unaccustomed as I am to public speaking, I know you realize it is your duty, and you do it in this way of contribution.

HUGO. We can afford it – me, Iggy and Harry.

DES. Well, I –

DADA. All right, Desmond. It isn't expected of you yet.

HUGO. Does Michael ever come across?

DADA. Hubert, it's not 'coming across' when you send me or give me money – When you send it to your mother and I. You all learned your Catechism. Well, honour thy father and thy mother. And when you send me, thy father, money, your honour. Do you get me?

HUGO. We'll squeeze Michael a bit. He'll chip in anymore.

DADA. I want nothing of him. And, anyway if I wanted him squeezed, who would I get to do it? Who? Me! – Myself! – The old man! . . . (*They laugh.*) He's gone out, is he? Were you talking to him?

DES. For a while.

DADA. About me?

DES. No.

DADA. What was he saying?

DES. Nothing.

DADA. That's a highly intelligent way of talking. I bet he told you I was – Well, imagine. What else did he say?

DES. He just said ye didn't get on so well.

DADA. And that it's my fault? Get wise to him, he said, to me and your brothers. Well, I'm telling you now, you get wise to him, boy. He tried the same game with Ignatius and Hubert, didn't he? Yes. But they were too smart for him. Looking-down-his-nose act, sneering. Nobody can be right, only him. But I'll do for him yet. He knows a lot, I'm sure.

DES. But, I think, you've got him – well, a bit wrong. He's – Well, he's not too bad.

DADA. Amn't I saying he's an ungrateful tramp. Disrupting. After all I did for him. Amn't I telling you –

MUSH (*enters*). Where's Harry? Where's Harry? They're up at The Lion! They're here! – Where's Harry?

HARRY (*comes out of the kitchen, drinking a glass of milk. He remains deliberately casual*). Hah?

MUSH. The Mulryans. They're up at The Lion.

HARRY. Yeh?

MUSH. I was pointed out. And the first thing I know, the big fella, John, come over behind me and was saying, 'I'll have a pint, mate'.

HARRY. Yeh?

MUSH. I did. And he said, 'You a friend of the Carneys?' Yeh. 'You know where they live?' Yeh – Yeh. 'Well, run down and tell them, anytime.'

IGGY. R-r-r-right.

HARRY. No rush. They're drinking?

MUSH. He swallowed the pint with my compliments easy enough.

HARRY. Let them enjoy themselves a while, Iggy. How many of them?

MUSH. Six.

HARRY. Six?

MUSH. There's a rumour one of them is locked up.

HARRY. That a pity, Des? Not seven? (*To* MUSH.) An' yeh?

MUSH. The big fella, John –

IGGY. 'K-k-k-king.'

HARRY. Him they call 'The King'.

MUSH. Big flat nose.

IGGY. I'll s-s-soon flatten it more for him.

MUSH. He's well over forty. (HARRY *nods.*)

IGGY. I'll – I'll s-s-soon –

MUSH. But – Jesus! – I wouldn't like him squeezing my head. He'd give – Jesus! – your ears an awful chewin'. . . .

HARRY. Go up and say, right. But that I'm out at the moment, and we're waiting for me, and then we'll be up.

IGGY. N-n-n-no! They'll think we're afraid.

HARRY. Naaw. Let them think. They'll think different later. Say nine o'clock we'll be up, Mush, and we'll have a drink, and then ramble up to Rock's Lane.

MUSH. Aw, jay, sham –

HARRY. Go on.

MUSH. Couldn't Hugo go, or –

HARRY. No.

MUSH *exits.*

HUGO. What about the Killer?

HARRY. Naaw. (*Shakes his head at* HUGO.)

HUGO. Hah? We could bring him, like, for the crack.

HARRY. Naw-naw. (*Winks at* HUGO, *nodding behind* DES's *back.*)

HUGO. Hah?

HARRY. He's a spoiler! (*To* IGGY.) Tucks of time.

DES. What about a plan? Won't we line up in some special way, like in a 'V', maybe?

HARRY. None of us goin' writing books of memories later. The best time to think is when you see them across from you. Don't worry, Des, I'll harden your fists. And, Iggy, I have a –

IGGY. I'll m-m-manage without it.

HARRY. A handy chain.

IGGY. I'll m-manage without it.

HARRY. Five against six, maybe seven.

IGGY. N-n-no one is telling me. I don't have to use none of them things.

HARRY. Okay, it's your –

IGGY. M-m-my head.

HARRY. Okay.

IGGY. M-m-my head.

HARRY. All right.

IGGY. Right.

HARRY. Dada?

DADA. No equipment, thank you.

HARRY. Seems like ye're taking all this like a game. Ah, ye might change yere minds when ye see them. But, person'lly, I'm going to change. Hah? For dinner. I'm not spoiling this jacket. (*Exits and goes up stairs.*)

IGGY. Hurry up!

DADA. Listen, boys, we all seem to be fixed up all right. Remember, if there's clubs it'll all be over in a few minutes, so get into it right away. Fight for the name, and have valour. And – have valour, and united stand – divided fall. No bickering and – Get into it right away. (*Moves towards door.*) That old factory – Behind that – the one you pointed out to me this morning, Ignatius.

HUGO. Where are you going?

DADA. There's a little something I'd arranged about this fight tonight.

HUGO. But it's at nine –

DADA. Nine, yes. Plenty of time to get there if I hurry.

HUGO. Where are you going?

DADA. A secret, Hubert. My secret. A little surprise I'd arranged for you all. Behind the factory, nine, Rock's Lane, I have that. (*Exits.*)

IGGY (*calls*). Harry!

HUGO (*reflectively*). A surprise he arranged. I wonder what?

DES. Dada'll be there.

IGGY. Harry!

HUGO. Oh, he wouldn't miss it.

DES. The waiting is the worst, Iggy? I wish it was over.

HUGO. You're not getting afraid, are you?

IGGY. Not Des. (*Calls.*) Harry! H-h-harry!

HUGO (*sings*). 'Yummy-yummy-yummy, I've a pain in my tummy.'

HARRY (*off, roars*). Coming! Jesus!

IGGY (*to* DES). I'm always shivery too before anything happens. Shaky, not afraid, just shivery till the second it starts.

MICHAEL *enters. He goes to kitchen door and looks in. He is about to move out of room again.*

HUGO. She's upstairs, rocking the babbies to sleep.

DES. The Mulryans are up in The Lion. (*Pause.*) Six of them. Maybe seven.

MICHAEL. . . . Well, I didn't think ye had that much sense to stay in and keep away from them.

IGGY (*calling* HARRY). C-c-come on, sham!

HARRY (*off, coming downstairs*). Tucks of time, tucks of time.

MICHAEL. Surely, ye're not going?

HUGO. We was waiting for you. We love you to jine (*join*) us.

HARRY *enters. He has changed into his second-best clothes.*

HARRY. Aaa, how yeh, Michael! You got the news?

MICHAEL. I'm surprised Dada isn't here making speeches on this – auspicious, is it? – occasion. I thought it was him I saw hurrying away from the house when I was coming down.

HARRY *has been looking around for* DADA. *He looks at* IGGY. IGGY *shrugs. He looks at* HUGO.

HUGO. He's gone to get something he forgot. He'll meet us there.

MICHAEL. The next time you'll see him –

HARRY. He knows where?

HUGO. Yeh. Dada loves it.

MICHAEL. Take a tip from him and get lost the same.

HARRY. Hah? No, Michael. Out to get a few brandies in him he's gone.

IGGY. Are we r-r-right?

HARRY. Naaw, let Michael rip. I love being educated by a smart bloke.

MICHAEL. It's no use, Harry. The odds are too big this time. You know about them things. Seven to four now. Seven Mulryans. Not just seven ordinary yahoos just over. And look at all the things they've done in Birmingham for the past ten years. . . . I'm only for your good. . . . Well, have a bit of consideration. You're not taking him (DES) with you?

HARRY. Yeh?

MICHAEL. I'm only giving you a bit of advice.

HARRY. From experience.

MICHAEL. Ye're crazy. That daft father has ye all gone mad. Fighting Carneys! If ye were fighting for a job, even! – A woman, even! Can't you see there's no point. The whole thing is mad, wrong. . . . Well, what if ye win? What does it do for you? Where does it get you? What good is it?

HARRY (stage brogue). Oh, 'tis no good at-tall-tall-tall.

HUGO. At-tall-tall-tall.

MICHAEL (to DES). You don't have to go. They can't make you.

HARRY. Tell him, Des.

MICHAEL. Plain talking now. You can get killed. It's happened before.

HARRY. Yeh?

MICHAEL. You might be dead in an hour. Do you know what dead is? Dada wised up. You won't see him again till it's all over. . . . Look, the man is as daft, thick and stupid a man as ever lived, but not thick enough to stick his neck out.

HUGO. Why don't you close him up?

HARRY. Are you finished, Muscles?

MICHAEL. Tell him what happened in The Bower one night with one of the Mulryans.

HARRY. Oh, our kid hears things. You must be mixing with rowdies to be hearing things like that.

MICHAEL. Tell him that.

HUGO. It won't shake Des.

HARRY. I'll tell him. Yeh see, Des, one night, 'bout year or two ago, the long-distance Mulryans was up here, and a funny thing happened in The Bower. Some bloke fancied himself, some old eejit, and had a tussle with 'The King' and 'The King' bit off the clown's ear.

HUGO. Half it.

HARRY. Mulryan bit off half the clown's ear, and he carries it 'round with him all the time in a matchbox.

MICHAEL. And that's no yarn. That'll tell you what they're like.

HARRY. Naw, it's no yarn, but it don't affect our Dessie. I could tell him stories better than that about what we done. He's not like you, pookies. Eh, Dessie?

MICHAEL. Do you want him to finish up like the other Mulryan, the eighth one? – Maybe there were nine of them, but what about the eighth brother? What about him? Tell him that.

BETTY *enters*.

HARRY. What about him? Well, jibber, what about him? Tell the missus, tell sweet Bet-ty, the one that caught you on.

IGGY. L-l-let's go.

HARRY. Naaw!

HUGO. Naaw!

HARRY. Our intelligent brother wants it seven to three. Our intelligent brother is warning him to keep away from us trash. Well, mouth, what about the eighth Mulryan? You tell us.

MICHAEL (*to* BETTY). Go upstairs.

HARRY. Stay where you are, English Polly, or whatever your name is. Listen to Tarzan. Michael don't want Polly to see him running like always. After arguments with us he goes back to her and talks all night in bed about how brilliant he was telling us off.

MICHAEL (*to* DES). One of the Mulryans was found one morning in a canal. He was only a young lad, just come over. He was all tied up. Ropes and belts and stones on him to weigh him down. The police found him, but they never did anything. They were glad to be rid of him, same as they'd be glad to find you the same way. He was Mulryan, you're Carney. It's the same thing.

HARRY. Now, good man, you told him.

MICHAEL. Let him talk for himself.

HARRY. Go on, Des, tell him he's the colour of his daff.

IGGY. You're not afraid?

HUGO. Tell him.

DES. . . . No, I'm going – I'm not afraid of – no one. I never –

HARRY. Good, Des.

MICHAEL. Give him a chance. Ye don't tell him what to say. Des, look at it –

HARRY. Now, Mikey, you're getting more than a chance yourself.

DES (*nervous outburst*). No. I'm goin'! I'm not afraid of no one! I'm fighting with my brothers! I'm hearing a lot about brothers and helping and that for the last twenty-four hours. They're all against us! We'll get them! (*To* MICHAEL.) I think you should be with us too!

HUGO. Bring him, bring him, bring him for the crack!

HARRY. If Mikey come he'd be home before us to wet the tea.

IGGY. T-t-too much delaying. Come on, we'll get it over. (*Swaggers out, followed by* DES *and* HUGO.)

MICHAEL. Des!

HARRY (*pushes* MICHAEL *back*). Get out of it, jibber! We'll see you later. Maybe settle our person'l business 'bout the Muslims. Don't forget. And mind English Polly there.

Exits. Pause.

BETTY. What are you going to do?

MICHAEL. What do? Aw, you're asking me what am I going to do! What do you think I can do? And what's all this Polly act with you and Harry?

BETTY. I can't help it if your brothers are thick.

MICHAEL. Your own family isn't all that nice and respectable.

BETTY. Well, they aren't savages or madmen or – If my dad only knew how I was being treated –

MICHAEL. Your dad, your family! If they knew this, if they knew that! I know exactly what your family is like. Like Harry said, I was caught on.

BETTY *starts to cry.* MICHAEL *is sorry for what he has said. He wants to apologize, to put his arm around her. He can't. Pause.*

BETTY. It's no use trying to get them out. We'll have to move ourselves.

MICHAEL. Look at what they're doing to Des.

BETTY. It's done – It's done! He's the same as them.

MICHAEL. You don't know him right.

BETTY. He isn't worth it. You heard him, afraid of no one. You tried. You only remember him as a child. If he was older than you he'd be the same as the others. (*Pause.*) . . . I don't know. It seems such an easy thing to sit around a table and have a meal.

MICHAEL. Yes, they will.

BETTY. *They* won't. Never!

MICHAEL. It's only a stage they're –

BETTY. What about last night? 'We'll put him to bed like in the old days.' Does everyone go through that stage? And you had to leave the house.

MICHAEL. I hadn't. I was avoiding trouble.

BETTY. Here? Avoid trouble in this place?

MICHAEL. It was their first night over. What did you want to happen?

BETTY. You don't owe them anything, Michael.

MICHAEL. I know.

BETTY. Well then. You don't have to put up with them.

MICHAEL. I know! I always knew! . . . But they think I do now, since that *stupid* thing happened a few weeks ago. (*She looks at him.*) It's nothing. . . . Just, it's on my mind. . . . They don't let me forget it anyway. . . . Well, that night my coat was torn that I said I'd fell. I was coming home, and not so far up from here, these four darkies. I was just passing and one of them pushed me off the path. Said it was his right-of-way. I didn't say anything. Just started to go on. And then another one of them stood out in front of me and started to pull me about. And then I was in the middle of them, and I started shouting for help. I was in the middle of them, and they were pushing around, spitting on me, one of them saying, 'White spit out of black men'. And I kept shouting for help. And then I saw my three *thug* brothers running down the road to help me. Harry first, then Iggy and Hugo. And I saw Iggy flattening one of them. One blow. They were all fighting. Mad.

BETTY. What happened then?

MICHAEL. I ran. . . . It wasn't because I was afraid. I just don't believe in . . . Oh, God! . . . I stood for a second watching it all, and then I ran for here. . . . That was the only time in my life I knew my brothers were for me. I could have been near them that night. But well . . . I don't know. What's there to do? Harry was in hospital for two days after that night. I can't go and say, sorry, to Harry. . . . I wasn't afraid. I don't think I'm afraid of anything either. It was panic.

BETTY (*quietly*). No.

MICHAEL. What?

BETTY. No.

MICHAEL. It was –

BETTY. What do you want to do?

MICHAEL. What?

BETTY. I know you want something. I know I can't give it to you.

MICHAEL. . . . Oh, that's silly. That's – We're too old for that kind of talk. . . . Well, I want to get out of all this. And this awful feeling that something is going to happen me. I want to get out of this kind of life. I want Des – I want us all to be – I don't want to be what I am. I want to read. I don't want to say, 'Yes, sir' to anyone. But I can't get out of all this. I could have had a good job. I could have been well fixed. I could have *run* years ago. Away from them. I could have been a teacher. I had the ability. . . . What's wrong with me? . . .

BETTY. You can. You can make more of yourself. And they'll have more re – (*About to say respect.*) You'll have more influence over them.

MICHAEL. I know. . . . I could've run years ago, but who would be left with them? Who cared? Not *him*! He's sitting in some pub now, sucking a brandy, shooting his big mouth, hiding till this thing is all over.

BETTY. But what do *you* want to do?

MICHAEL. He's a great help now to his fighting sons.

BETTY. But what are you going to do?

MICHAEL. He's a great help to his army.

BETTY. But what are you –

MICHAEL. Well, I don't believe in his fighting Carneys. I don't believe in that game.

BETTY. It doesn't matter what you believe at the moment. You owe them something – you said it yourself. Don't start bringing your father or –

MICHAEL. What?

BETTY. I'm only trying to tell you stop and think for a moment. It's no good going from one thing to the other.

MICHAEL. I'll do the deciding about what's good and bad.

BETTY. Ah, I'm sick! You come crying your stories to me, and I listen –

MICHAEL. No one is asking you to –

BETTY. I'm sick to death! First Iggy, then Harry, then your father, then Des! – Des! – Des! And then you want something, and then you owe them something. I go to talk and I'm told to shut up. You won't put them out, you won't leave – what are you going to do?

MICHAEL. What do you want me to do?

BETTY. Fight!

MICHAEL. Fight! You know how I feel about –

BETTY. Fight! Fight! Fight! Do something! Fight anything! And then maybe we can –

MICHAEL. And won't that prove –

BETTY. Don't start it all over again –

MICHAEL. But wouldn't that prove to them after all my years' talking against it that –

BETTY. Fight! They'll think more of you. Respect you. I'll think more of you. If that matters anymore. We'll do something then. We'll go. Or they'll go. We'll have a better chance if you prove you're not a . . .

MICHAEL (*quietly, simply*). What? . . . Finish it.

BETTY (*crying*). I don't know what's happening, love.

MICHAEL (*quietly*). Jesus! . . . Jesus! . . . Prove I'm not a coward. (*Grabs a milk bottle.*) With a milk bottle, is it? Blood, and fighting, and light-heads, and daft fathers, and mad brothers! With this is it? (*Throws the bottle away and grabs a knife.*) Or this? Hah? Do you want me to use it? Hah? (*Throws the knife away.*) Right. Right then. I'm Carney too, another Carney. Right.

MICHAEL *exits.* BETTY *cries quietly.*

Act Three

A few hours later, DADA *is sitting at the table. He is drunk. A small 'elastoplast' (band-aid) on his forehead. On the table, two bottles of whisky, cups, glasses, and a small parcel. Through the following, he sings snatches of 'I hear You Calling Me'.*

BETTY *is standing at the front door, looking out. She moves in and out to the front door during the Scene.*

DADA (*singing*). 'I hear you calling me; you called me when the moon had veiled her light; before I went from you into the night, you spoke . . .' Beautiful song that. Not many can sing it. Lovely. 'Still here's the distant music of your voice'. . . . No use going in and out like that, ma'am. Relax. Take deep breaths. Deep breaths is the secret. Look. (*Inhales and exhales, admiring his chest expansion.*) See that? Now I'm completely relaxed. Whisky helps too. It relaxes the throat, the muscles. You have muscles in your throat, you know. . . . Yeah. All great singers have a couple of half-ones before they go out. You get the high notes then. (*Drinks, clears his throat, sings.*) 'I hear you calling me.' . . . Lovely. . . . Try a drop, ma'am? Put a bit of life in you. It's food, you know. No? Barley and rye and things. (*Raises his glass.*) As my brother, Father Kevin, used to say – Did Michael tell you I've a brother a priest, the foreign missions? . . . No? Well, I have! . . . As he used to say – (*Raises his glass again.*) Humanum est errare, there is truth in wine! (*Drinks. Pause.*) . . . Do you ever feel lonely? . . . I always thought I'd have a house with nice music. . . . Wha'?

BETTY. You could go out and look for them.

DADA. Don't worry, ma'am. Cross your bridges – when they come to you. (*Laughs.*) . . . Yeah . . . Any books in the house, good books?

BETTY. No.

DADA. Wha'? . . . None at all?

BETTY. No.

DADA. Doesn't he read? It's education to read. This wouldn't be my house. At home I've two rooms full of books. Valuable. Worth a thousand – more – a few thousand pounds. Wouldn't sell them.

I have! They can't be got at all now. Did you ever read *The History of Ancient Greece,* did you? I'm reading that now, just before I came over. Very interesting on how . . . Yeh. Did you ever read *True Men As We Need Them*? . . . No . . . I bet you never read *Ulysses*? Hah? – Wha'? – Did you? No. A Dublin lad and all wrote *Ulysses.* Great book. Famous book. All about how . . . how . . . Yeah . . . Can't be got at all now. All classic books like them I have. No Buck Jones stuff for me. . . . He used to read one time. Doesn't he now?

BETTY. No.

DADA. No. . . . Do you think he's intelligent?

BETTY. No – Yes.

DADA. Do you?

BETTY. I do.

DADA. Well, I don't. . . . He doesn't read, you said! Like, he – Well, he isn't a good conversationalist. Like, well he – Well, there's more caffeine in tea than coffee. Caffeine, the drug, you know. (*Pause.*) . . . You were a clerk once, weren't you? . . . Michael said you were. . . . Nice clean job. . . . Did he ever tell you I was a guard once? Did he ever tell you I was a guard, a policeman?

BETTY. No.

DADA. No. He wouldn't. No. . . . Well, I was! . . . A lot of clerical work attached to that. . . . But they – No, I didn't like it anyway. Packed it in. I resigned! . . . Does he be talking about me?

BETTY. He never talks about you at all.

DADA. N-a-a-a-w! . . . He thinks he knows it all. But he doesn't know much about life. Very smart. Very – very – very smart. (*Drinks, pauses, sings.*) . . . 'Do you remember me standing there? For one last kiss, beneath the kind stars' light.' (*Drinks, pause. Suddenly.*) . . . I hate! I hate the world! It all! . . . But I'll get them! I'll get them! By the sweet, living, and holy Virgin Mary, I'll shatter them! They accepted me. They drank with me. I made good conversation. Then, at their whim, a little pip-squeak of an architect can come along and offer me the job as caretaker. To clean up after him! But I'll – I'll – Do you hear me? I hate! . . . (*Grows softer.*) Oh, I wish to God I was out of it all. I wish I had something, anything. Away, away, some place. . . . No. No! I'm proud. I did all right by my family. Didn't I? . . . Yaas! (*Passionately to himself.*) On my solemn oath I did my best. . . . My best, my best, my best. I'm proud of them. Yah – yah – yah! I hate! (*Looks up and sees* BETTY *watching him. Softly.*) . . . Sit down, ma'am, can't you. Do you ever feel lonely?

BETTY. Michael talks like that sometimes when he –

DADA. Aw, Michael – Michael – Michael! Is that all you can say? Did he tell you not to listen to me? I talk through my hat?

BETTY. No.

DADA. You think he's great, don't you?

BETTY. Yes, I think – I –

DADA. Oh, don't mind me. I'm daft, stupid. But you think he's great.

BETTY. Yes. Yes! I do!

DADA. Well, he's only a shit! Now do you know? Do you know now? That's what he is!

BETTY *goes out to front door. Men's voices off.* DADA *pulls himself together and goes out to the door to meet his sons.* IGGY, DES, HUGO, MUSH *and* HARRY *enter,* DES *swaggering like* IGGY. *They carry marks of the fight – nothing extreme.* MUSH *possibly, looking the worst; pale and shaken.*

DADA. } Ah-haa! . . . Ah –
BETTY. } Where's Michael? . . . Where's Michael? . . .

DES. (*We*) Slaughtered them.

DADA. No need to ask how it went! Aha! No better men!

BETTY. What did you do with him?

HUGO. Your man's face after the chain.

DADA. Ah-haa! I have the drinks laid in. Come on.

BETTY. Where is he, Des?

DES. Don't be annoying me. Dada, Iggy made a right job of 'The King'.

DADA. Man, Ignatius! Drinks, boys!

HUGO. Mush wasn't supposed to be in it at all, but he got in the way of . . . (*They laugh.*)

MUSH (*pushes his chin out at* HARRY). Here, break your fist off that and report yourself sick. (*They laugh.*)

IGGY. They wasn't expecting the chain.

DES. And, Dada, I got this fella such a clout –

HUGO. When the fight was over, Des gave one little bloke, that was just standing watching, a terrible dig in the head.

DES. He's roaring yet.

IGGY. Naw, they wasn't expecting the chain.

DES. Aw, but did ye see the way the crowd pulled back to let us out? A kind of silence, fright, respect, they had.

HUGO. There was no one making passageway to let out the Mulryans.

IGGY. They wasn't expecting the chain. It's not the same winning that way.

DES. Naw, Iggy, naw. We won. We got revenge for you, Mush, didn't we?

HUGO. Aw, Jays, Mush moving across, just before it began, and Mulryan drew out – (*They laugh.*)

MUSH. I was going to – (*The laughter drowns him.*)

DADA. Good man, Mush.

MUSH. Well, the last fella I hit, I hit him such a blow that he used fall at the same time every night for a fortnight. (*They laugh.*)

HARRY. Have a drink, Betty. Come on, jine us.

BETTY. Where is he, Harry? He went out right after you, to help you.

DES. I seen him, Betty. There he was in the middle of it, flattening all round him.

HARRY (*to* BETTY). Yeh? Went out? That so? (*To the others.*) Hear that? (*To* BETTY.) You wouldn't be making things up now, like, so we'd be nice to him?

HUGO. You couldn't be up to Bitchey. Ye're well met, Michael and yourself.

HARRY. But come on, Betty, jine us.

HUGO. He's a traitor, that's what he is. Isn't he, Dada?

DADA. Drink up, boys. In with the Mulryans, that's the place you'd find him.

BETTY. And where were you tonight?

DADA. . . . What do you mean?

BETTY. Did you help them?

DADA. Oh, this is serious now, ma'am. I see. My fidelity is in doubt. Where was I? Is that your question? Boys? . . . You see, my sons, my own haven't the audacity, but I must answer you, a stranger. And a stranger I know nothing about!

HUGO. She has no right – (DADA *silences him.*)

BETTY. All I want to know is where is he. He did, really, go out after you.

DES. Maybe he did.

HARRY. What?

DES. Michael?

HARRY. Out to fight with – ? Michael won't hardly mix with us outside. He's a big shot, good boy, messenger boy.

DADA. Correct, Henry.

DES. Naw. You're wrong.

HARRY. Are you telling me?

DES. You have to think these things out. You see, with Michael –

HARRY. You're explaining to me?

DADA. Desmond, Michael looks on us –

HARRY. Stall now a minute. He's going *explaining* to me.

DADA. I'll explain.

HARRY. Hah? *You're* explaining too?

DADA. Henry, I said –

HARRY. No-no-no-no. He's going to tell me how I can't think things out.

DADA. It's bad manners to interrupt.

HARRY (*considers for a moment*). . . . Right. Just one question of you so first. Just one –

DADA. Desmond is under the misconception –

HARRY. Desmond is under a lot of things, but one question of you first. Like she said, where were you?

BETTY *goes out to the front door.*

DADA. . . . Do I –

HARRY. *I'd* love to know.

DADA. Well, I'm coming to it, Henry. . . . Gentlemen, we are having a dual celebration tonight. Not just one victory, but for my victory too. . . . Yes! (*Taps the band-aid on his forehead.*) Ah-haa, ye weren't the only battlers! You know wild horses wouldn't have kept me from the Mulryans tonight.

HUGO. Did something happen?

DADA. Did something happen? Wait'll you hear. Remember when I left here tonight?

HARRY. I was upstairs.

DADA. Well, Henry, I hit for a certain place to get this. (*Takes up the small parcel off the table.*) The surprise, Hubert. And then I said I'd have two drinks – Now, only two, mind – in the – what's this you call the pub? The – The – Oh, it doesn't matter. I got this little batch of stuff there too. (*The whisky.*) I came out, and I was making my way for Rock's Lane, and I got a bit lost for a while. But don't mind that so much. Anyway, I found myself in this darkish laneway, and all of a sudden, there's a fella stepping out in front of me, out of nowhere. Out of nowhere, he's beside me. 'Got a light, mate?' he says, kind of sizing me up. I suppose I look the wealthy type. 'Sorry', I said. I was out before, you know. 'Got a fag?' he said then, still in front of me. 'Out of the way', I said, pushing him out of my way. Then I saw this other fella hurrying towards me, and I heard a noise behind, and wasn't there a third guy sloping up on me as well.

DES. Like the Mulryan fella tonight when –

IGGY. Three of them, was it?

HUGO. Quares, was it?

DADA. Makes no matter what they were or wanted, but they were out for me, and I knew it.

HUGO. Yeh?

IGGY. Maybe someone we had a tangle with and they knew you.

DADA. I thought of that, Ignatius. But, anyway – Henry – I got my back to the wall and it started. Ah-haa, there's power in the old man yet! The first fella seemed to go mad when he saw I wasn't going to take it sitting-down style. He charged at me – Oh, a right lunatic! 'I'll swing for you!' he shouted.

HUGO. What did you do?

DADA. I swung for him! (*They laugh.*)

IGGY. Did she go down?

DADA. Like a sack. He didn't get up neither.

DES. Where was all this?

DADA. The other two came at me. I got a right one here in the jaw. Still sore. I thought I was gone. It isn't swelled, is it?

HUGO. Naw-naw – Go on, Dada.

DADA. And a right one in the forehead. I thought the plaster would help. Ah, it didn't really need it. Just a bruise.

IGGY. The other two. What did –

DADA. You see, one of them made this kick at me, and I part
ducked it. But I said then, all right, if that's the way ye want it.
And I lashed and kicked and kicked and lashed. I suppose the
same was happening to me, but I never felt it.

IGGY. Aw.

DADA. But I put the second fella across the road, he hit the wall,
and down.

IGGY. Did you put the three of them away?

DADA. No. No. I was nearly away myself. After the second fella I
got this kick, right here. (*Feels his groin.*) And lucky thing for me,
the third guy wasn't too anxious 'cause I was bunched. Anyone'd
be. And the pain, and winded, you know. And I started to get
away quick as I could, and when I got to the main street, I had
to throw myself on a seat there. Lord, I was bad, but I didn't care
who was looking. Sick as a dog, bunched completely, not worth
two-pence. And I couldn't stir, I'm telling you. Not for hours. . . .
I'm not as young as I was, boys.

HUGO. Talking about a night!

DADA. But I knew ye wouldn't let me down. The Carneys for it!

HUGO. Three of them! God! I'd love to have seen you in action.
And that little bitch out there was on to you. And when we should
have been with you. (*Calls.*) Hey! Hey you! Asking where he was.
Come here if you want to know!

DADA (*unwrapping the parcel*). Leave her; she's not worth it.

HUGO (*shouts*). Dada always has a good excuse!

DADA. I'd arranged in my mind to get this. A little surprise. (*The
parcels contains a small silver-plated cup.*) What do ye think of that?
That's what I had arranged to get.

HUGO. Lord, it's the real thing.

DADA. A gesture.

DES. Show it here.

MUSH. Smashing.

DADA. Gesture.

HUGO. That's valuable.

IGGY. Aw.

DADA. Don't mind the cost. Only the best is good enough. That's silver. Give it to me. We'll do this right. Henry. I'll present it proper. Properly. I present ye, Carneys, with this cup – trophy – magnificent trophy – for your courage and bravery in the face of the enemy. Outstanding. Ye fought bravely and well, and with indomitable courage – indomitable courage, and ye – ye fought bravely and well. Ye kept the flag flying high and ye – ye fought bravely and well. Here, you take it, Henry. I present it to you (DADA *and* HARRY *are looking at each other.*) . . . The captain – the general . . . A gesture from an old man.

After another moment, HARRY *accepts it silently.*

DADA. Congratulations! Good man, Henry! Great lads! Aw, ye're great lads! I'm proud of ye! Champions of England! Great Irishmen! The Carney name will be known all over! Stout-hearted men!

MUSH. From the County Mayo.

IGGY. Aw.

HUGO. Give us that one, Dada.

DADA (*false reluctance*). Aw, no.

MUSH. Go on, Mr Carney, a song.

DADA. Aw no.

HUGO. We'll make a right party out of it. You give us a song, Mush.

HARRY. One of your own make-ups, Mush.

HUGO. The one about Harry.

MUSH. I've a new one wrote.

DES. Who about?

MUSH. Iggy. Will I give it?

HUGO. In t'it.

HARRY. Silence now. One voice and one voice only.

MUSH (*produces a slip of paper and recites*).
   Iggy the Iron Man.
   I knew a great big noble man,
   His name was Iggy Carney;
   He was big and strong, could sing a song
   Could –

HUGO. Iggy can't sing.

IGGY. Shush!

HARRY. On, Mush.

MUSH. He was big and strong, could sing a song,
   Could lift the stone of Blarney;
   His hands was big and hard and swift,
   They really were quite mighty;
   And them that stood again' that bloke
   Was soon put out of sighty.

   When Iggy crossed the Atlantic foam
   To England's foggy dew,
   His name had swam before him
   And all the tough-uns drew;
   They tried to take his crown from him
   But in the end they ran,
   The hair oil scalding their cut-up heads,
   Away from the Iron Man.

   Oh, Iron Man, Oh Iron Man, we proudly sing thy name;
   If Brian Boru let us down, thou kept up Erin's fame;
   Thou beat and blackened men galore for the sake of liberty,
   From the dear old glens in sweet Mayo
   To the shores round Coventry.

   MUSH *is applauded. They cheer and laugh.*

HUGO. Good man, Mush!

HARRY. Give him another pint and fire him out!

Through the applause DADA *is standing in a corner with his back to them. He starts to sing. The noise subsiding, and they listen with considerable reverence.*

DADA (*sings* 'The Boys from the County Mayo').
Far away from the land of the shamrock and heather,
In search of a living as exiles we roam,
And whenever we chance to assemble together,
We think of the land where we once had a home.
But those homes are destroyed and our land confiscated,
The hand of the tyrant brought plunder and woe;
The fires are now dead and our hearths desolated,
In our once happy homes in the County Mayo.
   (*Chorus*)
So, boys, stick together in all kinds of weather,
Don't show the white feather wherever you go;
Be each as a brother and love one another,
Like stout-hearted men from the County Mayo.

   (DADA *is applauded.*)

If only I had accompaniment, piano.

HARRY. Quiet now again for Mush.

HUGO. A song now, Mush.

MUSH. Aw, don't be asking me after a singer like your father.

DADA. Try something anyway, it doesn't have to be as good.

IGGY. Naw, give's 'Harry from the Land of Saints and Scholars.'

DES. Is there none about me?

MUSH. No, I'll sing –

DES. Seems like you've them all about the others.

HARRY. Ary, don't mind him. Give 'Harry from the Land of –

DADA. Gentlemen! I propose we drink a toast. We'll drink to ourselves, the Carneys, on this memorable and momentous victory over the Mulryans, on this historic day – night – the twenty-fourth ult., nineteen hundred and –

MUSH. Inst.

HUGO. Hah?

MUSH. You should've said inst., not ult.

DADA. Mr O'Reilly is trying to tell me, boys, that I should have said inst. instead of ult. People, instead of saying the name of the month, for short they say –

MUSH. Inst.

DADA. Ult.

HUGO. Ult! Ult!

MUSH. No, he should've said –

DES. Close it! (*Your mouth.*)

HUGO. Ult!

MUSH. Hah? (*Nervously.*) Hah-haa!

DES. You might be able to fool the others a bit, but not me. (*Looks round to see if the rest of the family is watching him.*) What do you mean, anyway, interrupting?

MUSH. I was only trying to –

DES (*hits MUSH*). Well, don't be 'onlyin',' d'yeh hear?

HARRY (*advising MUSH*). Cobblers, Mush. Lesson number two.

DADA, IGGY *and* HUGO *are laughing.* DES *laughs and starts to pursue* MUSH. MUSH *bolts for the door and escapes,* DES *missing him with a kick as he exits.*

MUSH (*off*). Tinkers! Carneys! Tinkers! Tinkers!

DES *grabs a whisky bottle and dashes out after* MUSH. *He is heard breaking the bottle outside.*

IGGY (*to HARRY who remains motionless*). Let it go, sham. (*Calls after DES.*) Come back! Des! (*To the others.*) Mush'd bring the police awful fast. She's a terror for the shades when she's in trouble.

DADA (*laughs*). I was sure he'd be another Michael. Him and Michael when they were small, ye know –

HARRY. And when they was big too.

DES *enters, broken bottle in his hand.*

IGGY. Did you get her?

DES. Naw.

DADA. Good man, Desmond! He's nearly soused. He learns fast, doesn't he?

DES. Learning! (*Tapping his head.*) Up here you want it.

HARRY. There was still some –

DES (*pointing at his feet*). Down there for dancing.

HARRY (*tapping his head*). Up here in your arse. There was still some whisky left in that bottle.

DES. Ho-ho, learning! Anyone care to try me? Anyone? Anyone that likes? Any time?

HUGO (*laughs*). Any place.

DES. What are you laughing at? Do you think I wouldn't take you?

HUGO (*laughs*). I'm bloody sure of it.

DES. You stupid get!

HUGO (*jumps up. IGGY moves in between them*). Are you starting the superior game now? I'll burst your big head in. I'll make him sorry he ever came.

IGGY (*easing the bottle from DES*). Sit down, the two of ye. I thought we were celebrating.

DES. I did more than him in the fight, didn't I?

IGGY. Sit down, Des.

DES. Didn't you see the state I left your man in?

IGGY. We seen it.

HUGO. Let him go, and see the state I'll leave him in.

HARRY (*quietly*). Let them at it.

HUGO. Nobody is calling me a – names.

IGGY (*to* HUGO). Sit down. She's drunk.

HUGO sits. DES gets cocky again.

DES. Maybe you fancy yourself too, hah?

IGGY. Naw. (*Winks at* HUGO.) You'd take any of us.

DES. Well, like I said now, any of ye that wants it. (*About to sit, changes his mind. Then, into* IGGY's *face.*) Well, Iron M-m-m-man?

Split second pause, then IGGY *sweeps* DES *back against the wall and is up against him with amazing speed.* DES *flinches.*

IGGY. No more now. You shut up when I say to, or you'll have no mouth. Do you understand that? (*Short pause. Then* HARRY *laughs at* DES.) A sing-song! 'So-s-so, boys, stick together in all kinds of weather, don't show the white feather wherever you go. Be each . . .' (*Etc.*)

The others join in; DADA *providing a strange counterpoint with his Irish tenor* Oft in the Stilly Night. *Through this,* MICHAEL *has come in front door. He is drunk.* BETTY *has tried to persuade him not to join the party. He enters the room, followed by* BETTY. *He stands there for a few moments before they notice him.*

HUGO. Look!

HARRY. We won, Michael, you'll love to hear!

IGGY. I wonder had she much to drink?

HARRY. Ten points while the Angelus was ringin'. Give us an auld warble, Michael.

DADA (*sings*). 'Oft in the Stilly Night, ere slumber chains have . . . '

IGGY. Give her a drink.

HARRY. Sing for Des. You like Des.

HUGO. Sing for Betty.

HARRY. Poor disappointed Polly – (*To* BETTY.) Keep out of it, English Polly! We won, Michael, you'll love to hear. But we just want you to know we just turned over a new leaf. And we come to the conclusion that Des is going back to Mary Horan's country. And Hugo is going to the university, and I'm going paying for his fees. And Iggy is going joining the Foreign Legion of Mary. And Dada is going off, with his old one-two, killing communists. And I'm going joining the nuns.

BETTY. Let's go upstairs, Michael.

HARRY. No-no-no-no-no, wait'll you hear –

BETTY. We don't want to hear!

DADA. Don't be unsociable, ma'am.

BETTY. We've heard enough.

HUGO (*giggles*). Upstairs.

DADA (*sings*). 'Sad memory brings the light of other days around me . . .'

BETTY. Come on, love. (MICHAEL *pushes her hand away.*)

HARRY. See what I mean? That's what I was going to say. He's a killer at heart. Ask any of the lads. Even when we was small –

HUGO ⎱ World Champ Carney –
HARRY ⎰ Do you know what he'd be at, Polly? Off strangling asses in the morning before his breakfast. Just for practice. Yeh. That's right. And he'd be –

BETTY. Stop it! Stop it! We don't want to hear any more.

HARRY. But we just want some more advice.

BETTY. You're not funny!

HARRY. She don't understand, Michael! Look, we have a party in the family. Our victory. What do you say? Look: happy family, brothers stickin' together in all kinds of weather.

DADA. Don't show the white feather –

HARRY. Michael never shown that.

DADA. No.

HUGO. No.

DADA. Ignatius?

IGGY. Aw.

DADA. Desmond?

DES. Well, maybe we should –

HARRY. Yeh?

DES. Like, well, make it up now. Like, it would –

HARRY. Yeh? . . . Like? . . . But person'lly, I wouldn't like to tangle with the ass-strangler.

MICHAEL (*drunkenly, smiling, to himself*). This is your victory party?

HARRY. Shh-shh-shh-shh, the advice is coming. Yeh? (MICHAEL *shakes his head, muttering to himself.*) . . . Hah?

BETTY. Come on, Michael.

MICHAEL (*smiling*). Who are you coddin'? Your victory party.

HARRY. Hah?

BETTY. Leave it, Michael.

HARRY. Hah?

BETTY. Come on, Michael.

HARRY. No, I don't think he's saying congratulations –

BETTY. Stop it!

MICHAEL. Is this your victory party over *them*?

HARRY. No, I don't think he's saying well done. I don't think he's –

BETTY. Stop it!

MICHAEL. Over *them*?

DADA. See him sneering? Don't take it off him.

HARRY (*to* MICHAEL). Hah?

BETTY. Stop it! Stop it! Stop it! You all must get out of here now! You must! Now! We don't care where you go! You must leave us! All of you.

MICHAEL. Keep out of it.

DADA. Who's talking? The woman? The stranger?

HARRY. No, Michael is going to throw me out.

BETTY. We've had enough!

HUGO. Aaa, Betty me love – (*Pushes her on top of* MICHAEL.) Michael is going to throw me out.

BETTY. Pigs! Pigs! You're only pigs! Animals! That's all you are. (*Takes* MICHAEL's *arm. He pulls free of her.*)

HARRY. Yis?

MICHAEL (*to* BETTY). No, you don't belong to this great victory party over *them*.

DADA. What's he saying?

BETTY (*to* DADA). You should have more sense, than having them go on like this.

DADA. Ha-haa, boys!

MICHAEL (*to* BETTY). Go upstairs.

HARRY. Yis?

HUGO (*giggling*). Upstairs.

MICHAEL. And fester all night over *them*. And if you can do that, you'll be allowed join in the next victory party we have over *them*.

BETTY. Come on, love, please. (*She is tugging at his arm.*)

DADA. Listen to him, boys.

HUGO (*giggling*). Love. Love.

BETTY. And if you don't go – If you're not gone in the morning – We'll – We'll have you out. We'll –

MICHAEL. I said keep out of it.

HARRY. Yis-yis-yis?

BETTY. We'll call the police.

MICHAEL. I said keep out of it.

HARRY. Yis-yis-yis?

BETTY. Please, Michael, please, love, come on, please. . . .

HARRY. Yis-yis-yis? (MICHAEL *pulls his arm free, and hits her. Triumphantly.*) Yis!

MICHAEL *and* BETTY *stand looking at each other. The others are laughing.* BETTY *exits upstairs.*

DADA. Ha-haa, boys!

MICHAEL. You dirty hypocrite.

DADA. First, he nearly threw us all out; then, he hit the poor little missus.

MICHAEL (*quietly*). The years I saw how you treated Mama. (*They continue laughing, refilling their glasses, etc.* MICHAEL *watching them. Quietly.*) Your poor, big, stupid mouths.

IGGY. Aa, who a-a-are – do you think you're talking to?

MICHAEL. All your poor, big, stupid, ignorant mouths.

IGGY. You didn't get so far with all your clever ways!

HARRY (*first realization*). Hah? That's right!

DADA (*first realization*). That's right! Good lads!

HARRY. All his big talk and he's no bank manager nowhere.

DADA. He didn't do so well after all, did he? No!

MICHAEL. If I had –

HARRY. Aa, Mikey boy, if-if-if! If you got a chance, is it?

IGGY. Give her another chance to hit Betty again.

HARRY. If your head wasn't so big, is it?

MICHAEL. If I could have got away from ye!

HARRY. If you weren't so handsome, like. All them other managers got the breaks, 'cept you.

DADA. If Hugo got a chance he'd be a scientist, making –

HUGO. Bombs, Dada, bombs!

HARRY. Now, I find that very interesting about you. And poor Des got no chance neither. Only for us he would. Tough that.

MICHAEL (*goes to* HARRY). If I had got away from things like ye!

DADA. Don't take it off him, Henry –

HARRY. Stall. (*To* MICHAEL.) What?

MICHAEL. Anything else to say tonight? . . . Anything else to do?

HARRY. Hah?

MICHAEL. To make you happy. To get it all off your chest.

HARRY. . . . Ah . . . yeh. Yeh. I agree with you about everything. You're real intelligent and I'm not, and you're always right, and I like that. Even about Mush and things. And I agree you'd never see a fella stuck, like, old stock. And the evening you were passing with some respectable bird one time, and I was standing outside the cinema, and I don't think you mustn't have seen me at first 'cause your eyes just flickered and you walked right past and didn't say hello. But then – I didn't understand it. But I feel a few other lads standing round the cinema did, 'cause they smiled. And you said to her, ''scuse me', and you come back to me, sort of serious stranger, never said a word, slipped me a tanner, so I could go in and be hid from view. Remember that?

MICHAEL. Anything else?

HARRY. Hah? . . . Yeh. I 'preciated that favour. And you'd never run, say, if your old buddies was fighting for you, like. Hah? Isn't that it? That's it. Yeh. Pals. (*Turns away from* MICHAEL. *Then he turns back, his fists clenched to hit* MICHAEL. MICHAEL *has expected this, and stands with his hands at his sides.* HARRY *pauses momentarily, then punches* MICHAEL *in the stomach.* MICHAEL *slumps to the floor.*) Isn't that it! – Isn't that it! – Isn't that it!

MICHAEL. God, ye're so – so – so –

HARRY. Thick! (*Kicking* MICHAEL.)

MICHAEL. Thick!

DADA. Do ye hear him, lads?

HARRY. Yes, we're so thick, stupid, twisted, thick! Oh, Michael, you are such a bright boy.

DADA. Haha-haa! The bright boy! Look at him now!

HARRY (*turns on* DADA). But that's what you think, isn't it? All us others in the family was thick, but he was bright boy.

DADA. I never – No, never said that, Henry.

HARRY. But you thought it.

DADA. Me? Him? I thought him intelligent?

HARRY. Yes, yes, yeh, you! You never said it, but it was there.

DADA. But-but-but, he's the flop in the house.

HARRY (*a plea*). But mean it, mean it!

DES. Michael got a better education, Harry, than –

HARRY. If I say a thing I'll mean it, I'll fight for it. No old crap talk, nor not knowing where I stand, nor –

DADA. Yes, he's no bank manager, Henry. He's no –

HARRY (*to* DADA). Or 'little surprises' from others. (*The silver cup.*)

DES. Michael was two years at the secondary school in –

HARRY. Keep quiet, you, I'm not so keen on you neither. Person'lly, I don't mind a man, no matter what he talks, if he means it, and you can see it, and if he'll stand up for it, and if he's – faithful.

DES. I was only pointing out –

HARRY. What's the money doing in your top pocket? (DES's *hand goes to his top pocket.*)

HUGO. He made out he'd none tonight when we was buying.

HARRY. That's all right – that's all right.

DES. I didn't want you to think that I –

DADA. Money, Henry? Where did he get it?

HARRY. I know where he got it. That doesn't matter. Faithful. I could admire he saying he's no money. It's the other – the – the other things – the – the –

DADA. Implications, Henry.

HARRY. Things! He doesn't think we can think straight. The things that's behind him. The things – where does he stand? Getting fed two sides, like. The sort of – the – the –

DADA. Implications.

HARRY. *Things!* (*He kicks a chair.*)

DADA. I understand –

HARRY. No.

DADA. I –

HARRY. No.

DADA. Actions have roots, I can explain.

HARRY. No! Not to me. No explaining to me. Things are clear enough to me. There's been so many good intelligent blokes for so long explaining things to thick lads. So many. So worried. All them clever blokes, cat smart, so worried about it all. (*Points at* MICHAEL.) He's so big and bright, he talks about families and home and all, and he's ashamed of us. See him apologizing to Betty when he invited us here. Little jokes for all, so she could take us. And all the time he doesn't know me outside. The preacher. Family. Home. (HARRY *is suppressing tears.*) But I'm thick. Thick lads don't feel, they can't be offended.

MICHAEL *pulls himself up off the floor.*

DADA. Yes, yas, yas, that's him all right! That's –

HARRY. No! Not *you*! I'm talking now. (*To* MICHAEL.) You worry about me, don't you? And then you apologize to them with the lovely white collars for me, don't you? And to them with the lovely white collars you say, 'Yes, sir, I'm a pig, sir, if you say so, sir!' And be pleased, 'cause they're surprised, smile to you, your manners, a pat on the head to a dog. And then you're better'n me?

DADA. Yes, Henry, no pride. He'll bow and scrape, and –

HARRY. I'm talking. (*To* MICHAEL.) Yes! You're right there too! I did salute McQuaide once. But I'm not still tearing the head off myself, pulling off my cap to salute them shams. They kick, you salute, and then they pray for you. Pray for the poor dirty pigs over here, now and at the hour of our death.

DADA. Amen.

HUGO. Amen.

HARRY . . . Amen.

DADA. Ignatius?

IGGY (*quietly*). I know what's he's talking about.

Pause.

DES. Oh, I don't know. (*Wanting to assert himself.*)

HARRY. Yeh?

Pause.

MICHAEL (*to* HARRY). Anything else?

DADA. Look! He's still better than us.

MICHAEL (*to* DADA). I thought you made all the speeches?

DADA. My authority – My authority is – I endorse all Henry said. (*Viciously.*) I'll settle you yet.

MICHAEL (*to* HARRY). Are you happy now?

DES. Oh, I don't know. I'm not a fool around here. All this talk is inferiority –

HARRY. Aaa, inferior complex. I know about that one too. That's a very handy one always when any of us, the thick lads, says anything about the big nobs – crap faces.

DES. Not inferior complex; it's an inferiority complex.

HARRY. Hah?

DADA. Inferiority complex, Henry, that's right.

HARRY (*glances at* DADA; *then to* DES). You're another almost terribly brainy bloke. You explain to me too. Aa, but you're wider than Tarzan here. You wear the sure-I'm-only-a-young-lad-foolish-but-there's-no-harm-in-me look. You like my nouns-'n'-singulars?

DES. I – They – I – Hah? (*Starts to sway drunkenly.*)

HARRY. No-no-no-no-no-no-no-no-no now! Don't gam on drunk. That's another special act with some. Drunk, like. No one is ever drunk till he's out, out cold. Funny, a thick lad like me knowing them things. You like the ways I talk?

DES. Why?

HARRY. Nah now. I'm asking you.

DES. It's all the same to me how you talk.

HARRY. Hah? I like the ways I talk too. (*Laughs.*) You're not so drunk now, are you? I like the ways our Michael talks too. He's not drunk neither now. I think he should have been your daddy, I think he should have you then, 'cause he wants to look after you so much, and you like him. (*Pushes DES across at MICHAEL.*)

DES (*trying to laugh it off*). Aw, easy, Harry, Harry sham, easy.

HARRY (*pushes DES back at MICHAEL again*). Naw. But you're frightened now, not drunk. That's funny. You frightened too, Michael?

MICHAEL. Yes.

HARRY (*to IGGY and HUGO*). Look at them!

MICHAEL. Anything else?

HARRY (*smiles, shakes his head*). No. I'm happy now.

HARRY, IGGY and HUGO *are on one side of the stage*, MICHAEL, DADA *and* DES *on the other.* HARRY, IGGY *and* HUGO *are refilling their glasses.* HUGO *is looking for beer.* HARRY *is croaking to himself – non-singing voice – 'So, boys, stick together . . .' etc.* MICHAEL *starts to walk out of the room.*

DADA. Wait! Wait! Wait, you! Henry! Henry! Boys! . . . (*They all look around at him and find him standing on a chair.* DADA *is also trying to reassert himself. Now that he has got their attention he does not know what to say. Trying to think of something to say.*) . . . Ah-haa! . . . Ah-haa for the Carneys! No better men! (*MICHAEL starts to move off again.*) Wait! Wait, you! . . . Boys! . . . Boys, boys . . . World Champ Carney! Clear the room, furniture back! Wait, you!

MICHAEL. For Christ's sake!

DADA. Like in the old days. See who's the best man, Desmond.

HARRY. Or maybe, us three again' ye three?

DADA. All must obey me now. My authority. My authority. Orders. Abide by the rules, Henry. Get that chair back against the wall, Hubert.

HUGO. World Champ Carney!

MICHAEL. How come you were always referee?

DADA. Getting brazen again. Soon fix that. Referee – procedure – authority – has to be referee. You should remember this game well, Michael.

MICHAEL. For Christ's sake! And ye're all getting out of here in the morning!

DADA. Watch your language before me, boy.

HARRY (*laughs*). The three of them again' themselves.

DADA. Thank God, boys, I could always stand up and –

MICHAEL. Hit, belt, clout –

DADA. Yes!

MICHAEL. Children! Hit kids!

DADA. Could always stand up, boys, talk with the best.

MICHAEL. Hit children!

DADA. Never bad language, never swore.

MICHAEL. Coming home, vomiting brandy and porter.

DADA. Hasn't learned his lesson yet. Come on, boys –

MICHAEL. In a temper, sulking, after his conversations with the big-shot friends. 'We'll get them!'

DADA. No change in him.

MICHAEL. Pulling four little kids out of bed, two, three, four in the morning. And up on a chair. 'World Champ Carney! Ah-haa for the Carneys! We'll get them! Charge!' And we all belted into one another.

DADA. Three of ye! Three!

MICHAEL. And you still see nothing wrong with that?

DADA. But little Michael – our eldest, boys –

MICHAEL. And there's nothing wrong with this now?

DADA. Our eldest, boys, remember? Wouldn't fight!

MICHAEL. A ridiculous old man, still roaring on the chair!

DADA. Wouldn't fight! Ashamed of him! Dribbling, whimpering, like a mangy dog in a corner!

MICHAEL. What's wrong with you? Why always the –

DADA. Nothing wrong with me!

MICHAEL. Why always the act!

DADA. Nothing wrong with me. I reared a family –

MICHAEL. And look at us now!

DADA. Reared – family – reared – that could –

MICHAEL. Don't you know fathers don't have to gam on to their children the great men they are?

DADA. Made men of ye! – Proud! – Reared a family –

MICHAEL. Honest to God, Dada, I tried to love you. What do you want to keep this up for?

DADA. Hah-haa, he loves me! Loves his old man!

MICHAEL. Even though I saw through everything you did.

DADA. Hah-haa! He sees all! Loves me!

MICHAEL. The big talk! What you were going to do!

DADA. Never – afraid – shadow!

MICHAEL. How tough you are. Were. I never saw anyone carried away from you.

DADA (viciously). Yeh-yeh-yeh! But you know nothing! But you know nothing!

MICHAEL. And the big-shot friends –

DADA. You know nothing about it! Nothing about life!

MICHAEL. Anthony Heneghan and the doctors. And I heard them myself laughing at you. And they still are.

DADA. Yaa – Yaa – Yaa – Yaa!

MICHAEL. And you talk about pride! And you smoking cigars and drinking brandy with them and your wife on her knees scrubbing their floors.

DADA. Yaa – Yaa – Yaa – Yaa!

MICHAEL. Where's your pride, Dada?

DADA. Don't – Don't talk irreverence about your mother, boy!

MICHAEL. There's still nothing wrong with that?

DADA. D'ye hear him? What he's saying about your mother, boys? D'ye hear him? Now you hear this.

MICHAEL. Is it a speech?

DADA. Now you hear this.

MICHAEL. Sing *I Hear You Calling Me*.

DADA. Now you hear this –

MICHAEL. You were always heard – braying!

DADA. Now you hear this – Now you hear this! Now you listen to me – You listen to me and I'll tell you a thing or two. Now you listen when I talk . . . Now, I want you all to hear, 'cause I have something to tell everyone. . . . I'll tell you about life . . . I'll tell you all right about it . . . I'll . . . I'm going to . . . I have something to tell you all. . . . I . . . I . . . Boys . . . Ah-haa! . . . Ah-haa! . . . And . . . (BETTY *is heard coming downstairs. She enters dressed in overcoat and carrying a suitcase.*) Aha, the stranger, back to save the mouse, Ignatius! Desmond! Ah-haa, Hubert! Hubert!

BETTY. Are you coming with me or are you staying with them?

HARRY. Don't leave us, Mikey.

HUGO. Don't leave us, Mikey.

DES. Hit her, Mikey.

DADA. Ah-haa!

DES. Think of the children, Mikey.

MICHAEL, *bewildered, looking almost stupidly at her. He looks at* DES.

BETTY. Don't look at him. He's the nice young brother you told me about.

DADA. Ah-haa, Desmond!

DES. Who do you think you're talking to!

BETTY. Are you coming? Now.

DES. Who, Bitchey, do you think you're talking to? Watch it now. (BETTY *exits, taking her suitcase.* HARRY, DADA, IGGY *and* HUGO *follow her to the front door to cheer her departure.* MICHAEL's *hand on* DES's *shoulder, restraining* DES.) Bitchey! Polly! English trash! Whore! (DES *becomes conscious of* MICHAEL. *His first reaction is shame. He half-turns away; then he swings back.*) What are you looking at? What are you looking at me like that for?

MICHAEL *and* DES *are in tears – or at the point of tears. The others rush back to the room.* DADA *gets up on the chair.*

HARRY. Quickly – quickly – quickly! Something happening here with the two geniuses.

HUGO. They can't wait to see who's World Champ Carney.

DES. Don't come that game with me now.

DADA. What's he saying to you, Desmond?

DES. Nothing. Just looking at me. As if I was dirt.

HARRY. What you doing about it? Talkin'?

DES. Everyone seems to think I'm a bit of a fool around here tonight.

MICHAEL *makes a move to leave the room.*

DADA. Are you letting him go?

HARRY. I don't think Des is no good.

DES *pulls* MICHAEL *back.*

DADA.	Ah-haa! Up to him, Desmond! Show him, Desmond!
HUGO.	The cow's thump, Des!
DADA.	For the honour of the Carneys!
HARRY.	I don't think Des is no good!
DADA.	Ah-haa, the sneerer!
HUGO.	The old one-two! Come on!
IGGY.	Get it over with!
HARRY.	Des is no good!
HUGO.	Aw, the cow's thump!
IGGY.	Hit him!
DADA.	Hit him! Hit him! Hit him! (*Like a schoolboy,* DES *hits* MICHAEL *on the shoulder.*) Yaa-hah-haa! Man, Desmond Muck and trash! Again! Again! Keep it going!

DES *hits* MICHAEL *again, this time more squarely.*

DES. The mouse! Couldn't command a woman even! A flea even!

DADA. Into it! Go on! Dirt! Dirt! Filth! Dirt! Muck and trash! Scum! Tinkers! Filth! (DES *knocks* MICHAEL *with his next blow.*) Mister intelligent sneerer! We'll get them! Looking down their noses! On – on – on!

The others are cheering. DES *is pushed at* MICHAEL *again.* MICHAEL *throws him back.*

MICHAEL. Jesus, our victory over *them*! (*Grabs a bottle.*) Are ye happy now? (DES *is coming at him again.*) Look at him: another victory for us over *them*! You don't know how to live either. (*He hits* DES *on the head with the bottle.* DES *falls and is still. Silence.*) . . . Is he all right? . . . see. . . . Des? (*Examines* DES.) . . . Des? He's dead. (*Pause.*)

IGGY. What do we do now? Dada?

DADA. . . . Wha'? . . . Wha'? . . . Well . . . I mean . . . the chair.

HARRY. What?

DADA. I was up on the . . . Ye were . . . Ye were all . . .

HARRY. Who's ye?

DADA. I was up – Ye were all . . . Wha'? . . . I had nothing to do
with – Not my fault. . . . No, listen boys. Him! Michael. Look at
him. What kind of nature is in him? (HARRY *turns away from*
DADA *and joins* MICHAEL *beside* DES's *body.*) Always the cause
of trouble in the house. Right from the beginning. The disrupter.
(IGGY *joins* MICHAEL *and* HARRY.) Ignatius. Look at him.
The disrupter, Hubert. (HUGO *joins* HARRY, IGGY *and*
MICHAEL. DADA *is isolated in a corner of the stage.*) Hubert . . .
Wha'? . . . Boys . . . Ye're not blaming me. . . . No control over
it. No one has anymore. . . . Did my best. Ye don't know how
hard it is. Life. Made men of ye. What else could I have done?
Tell me. Proud. Wha'? A man must have – And times were hard.
Never got the chances. Not there for us. Had the ability. Yas. And
lost the job in the guards, police. Brought up family, proper.
Properly. No man can do more than best. I tried. Must have some
kind of pride. Wha'? I tried, I did my best . . . I tried, I did my
best . . . Tried . . . Did my best . . . I tried . . .

The curtain falls slowly through the speech.

A Crucial Week in the Life of a Grocer's Assistant

A Crucial Week in the Life of a Grocer's Assistant was first performed at the Abbey Theatre with the following cast:

JOHN JOE MORAN	Donal McCann
MONA	Nuala Ní Aodha
MOTHER	Máirín D. O'Sullivan
FATHER	Mícheál Ó Briain
MULLINS	Peadar Lamb
ALEC BRADY	Harry Brogan
MRS SMITH	Máire Ní Dhonaill
AGNES SMITH	Fionnuala Kenny
MR BROWN	Eamon Kelly
PAKEY GARVEY	Séamus Newham
MIKO FEELY	Desmond Cave
FATHER DALY	Geoffrey Golden
PENSION MAN	Edward Golden

Director Alan Simpson
Designer Brian Collins
Lighting Tony Wakefield

Spring. A street on the outskirts of a small town in rural Ireland.

We can see into the kitchen and John Joe's bedroom of Moran's house; this is followed by part of the exterior of the house next door which is a shop (an ordinary-sized house window from which the curtains have been removed, containing a few boxes of sweets; a sign-board over the shop window reads 'ALEC BRADY'). The set should suggest that these are two in a row of houses.

And there is a pump on the street from which the people get their water supplies.

For the scenes in the grocery shop and hay shed: a shop-counter is pushed on stage and a bed of hay represents the hay shed.

Unusual lighting suggests the unreality of the dream scenes: movement and speech become stylized and the characters become caricatures.

Scene One

Monday

A pool of unreal light, growing in intensity, gradually lights the bedroom. Off, a train is whistling impatiently. Someone is trying to force the window to break into the bedroom.

John Joe is dreaming. He is thirty-three. His attitude throughout the dream is childlike.

Mona climbs into the room through the window. She is in her early twenties. She is scantily dressed in a slip. John Joe, immobile with fear, awaits an explanation.

MONA. How yeh!

JOHN JOE (*gasps at the sound of her voice*). Ah!

MONA. Ah? – Ah? – Ah?

JOHN JOE. Mona! (*Then – again waiting for an explanation.*) Ah?

MONA (*drawing his attention to the whistling train*). This is your chance –

JOHN JOE. Ah! –

MONA. Your very last chance.

JOHN JOE. Ah! –

MONA. Even the buds touched by the frost are trying hard to do something.

JOHN JOE. What?

MONA. It's Spring.

JOHN JOE. Yes.

MONA. You have things to do.

JOHN JOE. Yes.

MONA (*provocatively*). You can do what you like.

JOHN JOE. Aa, stop, Mona, I'm very sleepy.

MONA. Tickle me and I will tickle you.

JOHN JOE. That poor window has always been stuck.

MONA. Excuses.

JOHN JOE. They say, they say you are not of our ilk.

MONA. I think it's because you're just afraid.

JOHN JOE. It's not because I'm afraid at all.

MONA. Then why – then why?

JOHN JOE. O-o-o-o-o, spring is upsetting me.

MONA. First we live and then we die.

JOHN JOE. First a kiss to strengthen me, for I'm still drowsy.

He lies back on the pillow, smiling, anticipating the kiss.

MONA (*bending over him*). John Joe.

JOHN JOE. Mona.

But the medals on the chain about her neck brush (or drop into) his mouth. He spits them away as he sits up in consternation; he jumps out of bed; he wears only a shirt. Off, the train is whistling more impatiently and running feet are approaching to apprehend him.

The medals are coming, the medals are coming! – Hail Mary, Holy Mary! – Jesus mercy, Mary help! – There's rich and poor and black and white, a label on God, a label on you!

MONA (*gives him a small 'hold-all' bag which she has found under the bed*). My suitcase is outside on wheels for away, on wheels for away on the puff-puff!

JOHN JOE. You're not too good for me at all.

MONA. Make haste, they're coming!

JOHN JOE. But where, where?

MONA. Away, away!

JOHN JOE. Away, leave: always the answer. I have to have something to put in the bag.

MONA. Quick, or it will be your last springtime!

JOHN JOE (*trying to put a chair into his bag*). It won't fit, it won't fit!

MONA. They're here!

JOHN JOE (*crying*). They won't let me go, they won't let me stay!

MONA. Quick, before you're thirty! Quick, get up, it's Monday morning!

MONA jumps out the window and is gone. JOHN JOE tries to follow carrying the hold-all and the chair: he gets stuck in the window.

JOHN JOE (*crying*). It's not just a case of staying or leaving!

The sounds of the running feet stop immediately outside the door. The door opens and MOTHER stands in the doorway.

Mo-o-o-na!

He sees MOTHER. He stops crying; he is merely terrified.

MOTHER. Lord, Lord, Lord! Where is he going? (*He shakes his head, meaning nowhere.*) The hold-all in his hand, the good chair displaced, the poor windy open that's always been stuck! And dressed like that!

He sees that he is not wearing his trousers; he retreats to the bed.

JOHN JOE. I was on'y –

MOTHER. Put down the good chair! –

JOHN JOE. On'y playing –

MOTHER. Replace the hold-all! –

JOHN JOE. On'y –

MOTHER. Cover your knees from the frost-bite!

JOHN JOE (*getting into bed*). On'y playin', Mammy.

MOTHER. Only playing was he? Now for ye! Disturbing the equilibrium, on'y playing! Off-to-America, that's where he was going! The liar, the rogue!

JOHN JOE. No, Mammy.

MOTHER. Leaving us here in the lurch. Deserting his mammy and daddy and uncle that's good to him. That's gratitudinous! That's the son I reared. The favourite child I lavished with praise, the plans I had for his economy; the spotless boy, in days of old, who was so nice and knew his place: now as bad, if not worse, than his brother before him.

JOHN JOE (*groans*). Frank, oh Frank!

MOTHER. I'd swear my oath that poverty is not good enough for him. Heeding that hussy of a clotty of a plótha of a streeleen of an ownshook of a lebidjeh of a girleen that's working above in the bank. And she putting nonsense talk on him. His brains are scattered! He's foolish. But to think that our sweat is no thicker than water! Aren't we all right the way we are? And what have them with the gold to do with us? Now or ever? Let them afford their toothpaste and cosmetics. Let them afford their love, with their clean long legs. We will stick to our own and the soot, as we did through the centuries. We have a love of our own, and we will keep it! Lord! Lord! Deserters!

JOHN JOE. No, Mammy. (*He buries himself under the bedclothes.*)

MOTHER. Traitors!

JOHN JOE. No, Mammy.

MOTHER. Will you get up, will you! Showing me up before nice people! Sweet Jesus Mary, are you getting up at all today, are you?

The unreal lighting changes through the last above speech until the whole is lit in beautiful Spring morning sunshine. MOTHER *is standing over* JOHN JOE's *bed. She has been trying to awaken him for some time.* MOTHER *is about fifty-five, big lined face, given much to grimacing to emphasize what she says; appearance is slovenly – she wears too many clothes, and these are drab and old; harsh in expression and bitter; a product of Irish history – poverty and ignorance; but something great about her – one could say 'heroic' if it were the nineteenth century we were dealing with. She now appears near tears, clucking, pulling at her hair, rubbing her thighs, biting her fist. But she does this every morning.* JOHN JOE *is moving restlessly under the bedclothes.*

MOTHER (*sighs*). Lord! . . . It's Monday morning! It's Monday

morning! What kind of a fooleen is he besides anyone in the
country? . . . Will you get up, will you! Tck! Do you know how
long I'm calling you? Do you know what time it is? (JOHN JOE's
head appears from under the bedclothes.) Are you that stupid from
the lack of sleep? Oh, but sure, coming in all hours.

JOHN JOE *opens his eyes; he cannot comprehend the situation; he is
looking intently at* MOTHER *awaiting an explanation.*

Lord above!

JOHN JOE (*gasps*). Ah?

MOTHER. All right, stay there **then**, John Joe, stay there. That's
the right thing to do. Don't think of others. (*Leaving the bedroom,
shouts.*) Get up will you! Sure, I'm mythered in the head myself
with him. The state he has me in here every morning!

JOHN JOE *gets up, dresses, etc. He looks at the hold-all which is
under the bed. He is not yet fully awake – nor does he attain that
condition until scene two.* MOTHER *is in the kitchen polishing his
shoes.* FATHER *is seated on a butter-box by the fire whistling
tunelessly to himself as he pulls on his old boots. There is a mug of tea
beside him. He is about sixty; he is given to trance-like staring at
nothing; his mood can change in an instant from one extreme to the
other.* MOTHER *is scarcely conscious of his existence.*
*There is a bath placed on two chairs in the centre of the kitchen; there
is a washing-board in the bath; and two or three bags of washing
waiting to be washed on the floor.*

MOTHER (*to herself*). Is he up? (*Shouts.*) Are you up?

FATHER *exits to rear of house, taking his mug of tea with him.*

Is he coming out? Are you coming out?

VOICE (*of* MULLINS *off, on the street*). We'll have snow! Hah?

And MULLINS *enters, carrying a bucket. This being a beautiful
morning 'We'll have snow' is* MULLINS' *idea of joke. He taps at*
ALEC's *window, then at* JOHN JOE's *window, calling brightly as
he does so:*

MULLINS. We'll have snow, Alec! . . . We'll have snow, John Joe!

And he continues to the pump to fill his bucket with water:

Hah? Hah?

MULLINS is in his late forties; he is a lonely man; very inquisitive; every sentence sounds like a question; staccato delivery. It is usual to hear MULLINS before seeing him which gives the impression that he is everywhere, seeing and hearing everything.

JOHN JOE comes from his bedroom to the kitchen. He puts on his shoes and sips his cup of tea.

MOTHER. Why didn't you put on your blue shirt? Oh, leave it so now, tck! Quick will you, hurry. Lord!

She exits to rear of house. She reappears almost at once with JOHN JOE's bicycle, wheeling it across the kitchen and out the front door. She pauses to check the pressure in the tyres.

ALEC has entered and is standing outside his shop window shaking tea-leaves out of a tea-pot. He is almost seventy, a proud, jaunty, old man; there is a touch of the bizarre about him in character and dress, though, at the moment, he is a little dishevelled, having just got up.

MULLINS (*at pump*). We'll have snow, Mrs Moran! Hah?

MOTHER. Morning. (*She sees ALEC.*) Good morning, Alec!

MOTHER *returns to kitchen.* ALEC *is following her.*

MULLINS. We'll have snow, Alec!

ALEC (*as he goes into Moran's*). Kiss me arse! (*He calls at JOHN JOE's room.*) Get up, you whore! (*Sees JOHN JOE in the kitchen.*) Oh, you're up. How are you off for tea, I haven't a grain in the house?

MOTHER. I'm down to the last quarter, but take what you want.

MULLINS *exits with his bucket of water from the road outside.*

ALEC (*putting tea in his pot; beaming*). Well, only eleven more shopping days before I start drawing the old-age pension! (*No response; MOTHER is sighing, watching JOHN JOE.*) . . . You're like the moon, Julia: down to the last quarter. (*No response.*) . . . Well, thanks, Julia. (*As he exits, returning to his shop*): Ah, the Monday mornings!

MOTHER. Couldn't you have said good morning to your uncle? Won't you hurry, will you! Will you move!

JOHN JOE *puts on his bicycle clips and goes out to his bike, followed by* MOTHER.

MOTHER. Couldn't you have said good morning to Alec?

JOHN JOE (*in direction of shop; dreamily*). Good morning, Uncle Alec.

MOTHER (*biting her fist*). Hurry will you. Hurry.

JOHN JOE *gets on his bicycle and starts to cycle off as* MRS SMITH *and* AGNES, *her daughter, enter. They are returning from Mass.* MRS SMITH *is about fifty-five; her voice is a crying, whining, poverty-stricken tremulo. If she laughs it is humourless. She is clutching her rosary-beads in her fist.* AGNES *is twenty-eight; she has ringlets. She carries her prayer-book in her hand, and she is chewing sweets unknown to her mother.*

MRS SMITH. Aaaaaa, the boy, John Joe! Off to work, darlin', now. The boy!

JOHN JOE. Morning. (*He exits.*)

MRS SMITH. Aaaa, morning! 'Tis, 'tis, 'tis indeed now, nice morning, 'tis, thank God, saints be praised, Blessed St. Joseph and St. Anthony, Mrs Moran, mmmmmmmm!

They have joined MOTHER *at Moran's door.* MOTHER *is now relaxed.*

MRS SMITH. We just heard. Mmmmm! Molly Byrne, the little poultry girl from the department. Dragged back to the hospital last night. Aaa now, let a young girl give a germ a chance! Saints protect us! Are you heeding every word I'm saying, Agnes, darlin'? And she was a civil little girl, but, I suppose, the company. More interested in pictures and dancing than staying in nights and getting on in the world.

MOTHER. And what is the matter with her?

MRS SMITH. Oh now, a lanna – (*Contemplates* AGNES; *as if* AGNES *were the victim.*) – Mmmmmm. Her breast. Mother of

God, wouldn't it frighten a saint, let alone any little girl, to be pulled out of your own little bed, and dragged away like that in the middle of the night? And when they took the clothes off the screaming child – Oh, little she wore but the nik-naks that's going now. Not a woolly vest to her back. And when they went further and opened her up – (*She notices that* AGNES *is not attentive.*) Well now, Agnes, if you're not going to heed your own mother you can go home ahead of me and think again about what you're proposing to do, and not be standing there limp, doing the cow on it, munchin'!

AGNES *exits.* MRS SMITH *looks after her, whining absently, tremulously.*

MRS SMITH. Crayture. (*Creature. To* MOTHER.) When the youth get the urge to do a thing! God help us! But, they say the hooter on the ambulance never screamed so loud before. And sure all knew the cheap-jack's son was her boyfriend for the last seven weeks. But they strapped the babe down on their tables, and when they opened her up, wasn't she red rotten. Cancer, my dear! Mmmmmm!

MRS SMITH *exits.* MOTHER *goes to kitchen and begins the washing.*

MULLINS (*off*). We'll have snow, Mrs Smith! . . . Hah? The poultry girl? . . . Hah? Hah? Hah?

Church bells off ring nine.

Scene Two

MR BROWN's *grocery shop. About 11.00 a.m.* MR BROWN *is looking out at the quiet street off. He is about sixty.* JOHN JOE, *wearing a shop coat stands behind the counter. They are sipping tea. Pause.*

MR BROWN (*to himself*). Quiet . . . But they're not in the co-op up the road either. People round here like the personal touch, the chat across the counter . . . They are not up in the co-op either, sir.

Footsteps off approaching. MR BROWN *waits expectantly. The footsteps pass the shop and fade.*

MR BROWN. Mrs Quigley.

JOHN JOE (*suddenly*). But it's a nice morning though, Mr Brown.

MR BROWN. If Horan's van comes this evening and I'm not here, only take the one side of bacon off him this week. There's no demand for it. (*Sighs.*) The money isn't circulating. (*Angry for a moment.*) The driver of that van is an awful harum-scarum. (*Pause.*) The money is not circulating, sir.

Pause. MR BROWN finishes his tea. He starts to move away; stops, thinks; then:

MR BROWN. Was that Lipton's tea?

JOHN JOE. 'Twas.

MR BROWN nods gravely and exits to rear of shop. Pause. Footsteps approaching. PAKEY GARVEY enters. PAKEY is home from England for his father's funeral. He is four or five years younger than JOHN JOE. His humour is bitter and cynical. He wears a three-quarter length mackintosh with epaulets. On his sleeve a black diamond to symbolize he is in mourning. JOHN JOE greets him eagerly.

JOHN JOE. Aw, jay, how yeh, Pakey! (*Then he remembers PAKEY is in morning; suddenly solemn-faced.*)

PAKEY grimaces cynically and sighs in an exaggerated way – and quite openly – at JOHN JOE's change of expression. He knows the rigmarole of sympathies that are coming. He plays along. He flicks his hand out of his pocket for the hand-shake.

PAKEY. How yeh, sonny!

JOHN JOE (*unsure*). I – I was sorry to hear about your father, Pake.

PAKEY (*sniffs*). I know that; everyone was sorry.

JOHN JOE. That's – that's the way.

PAKEY. That's the way, sonny.

Short pause.

PAKEY.   } I came in to –
JOHN JOE. } He lived –

PAKEY. What?

JOHN JOE. He had a good long – longish – life.

PAKEY. Oh, he had. Fifty-two, John Joe.

JOHN JOE. Jay, that's a lovely coat you have on, Pake.

PAKEY. What?

JOHN JOE. When are you going back to London, Pake?

PAKEY. Tomorrow morning. I've enough of the knockers and the craw-thumpers after four days in this place. Is 'His Holiness' in?

JOHN JOE. He's just gone out to the johns for a minute. (*Laughs.*) Eleven o'clock is his time.

PAKEY. Yes. I was looking at that messenger bike out there on my way in. Many's the trip I done on it for him. Remember? Seventeen-and-six a week he was paying me. But he used to give me time off for going up to the church for confession and that. 'Pray for the Russians, Patrick.'

JOHN JOE. Ary, he's all right.

PAKEY. If I was home in time my brother would not have ordered the coffin here.

JOHN JOE. How do you like London?

PAKEY. What?

JOHN JOE. Piccadilly, hah? Cricklewood for the crack. Tottenham Court Road. Camden town for the good lie down, and Hammersmith for dancing. Don't they have lovely names on places?

PAKEY. Were you ever – ?

JOHN JOE. No, but, you know. I meet fellahs like yourself, like, now and again, home on holidays.

PAKEY (*takes out a fat wallet*). Ah, sure, you have a good job here. (*He hands* JOHN JOE *two pay-packets.*)

JOHN JOE. What? £41–7–4? A week?

PAKEY. They used call me 'Bags' around here.

JOHN JOE. And what are you doing over there to be –

PAKEY. And they used call my father –

JOHN JOE (*reading second pay-packet*). £43–11–2 –

PAKEY. 'Rags'.

JOHN JOE. That's great money, Pake.

PAKEY. 'Rags' . . . But isn't it a wonder you never –

JOHN JOE. I never had any wish to leave.

PAKEY. I thought that must be it.

JOHN JOE (*phoney laugh*). Is it company you want over there?

PAKEY. Yeh?

JOHN JOE. No-no, I'll tell you. A few years ago, a few of us in
   Dublin one weekend, and I had half-a-mind to take the boat and
   – (*He makes obscene 'V' gesture.*) – the lot.

PAKEY. Yeh?

JOHN JOE. I nearly did.

PAKEY. Yeh?

JOHN JOE. I nearly – I – (PAKEY *takes back his pay-packets.*) But
   – but – but, tell me, tell me this, Pake, apart from the money over
   there –

PAKEY. Apart from *what*?

JOHN JOE. What I mean is . . .

PAKEY. Yeh? . . . I'm surprised at anyone born and reared in this
   holy town to make a statement like that. Ah, but they love the
   dead around here.

MR BROWN *enters, hurrying to* PAKEY, *gushing, hand out-
stretched.*

MR BROWN. Patrick! Patrick!

PAKEY. Malachy! Malachy! (*Deftly flicks out his hand again for handshake.*) I came in to settle up with you for the coffin.

MR BROWN. Well now, Patrick, you know I'm not worried about the bill. You know that now, don't you, Patrick?

PAKEY. Yes – yes, I know that well, Malachy, *But.*

MR BROWN. Nor was I ever worried in dealings with the Garveys.

PAKEY. Except the time –

MR BROWN. In dealings with the Garveys, sir.

PAKEY (*groans aloud, rolling his eyes up at the ceiling*). But – if – we – could, Mr Brown get down to –

MR BROWN. But wasn't it the sad journey you had to make?

PAKEY. 'Twas.

MR BROWN. 'Twas.

PAKEY. 'Twas.

MR BROWN. 'Twas. 'Twas indeed.

PAKEY. 'Twas. 'Twas, John Joe?

JOHN JOE (*trying to restrain his laughter*). 'Twas.

MR BROWN. It was, sir. (MR BROWN *realizes the mockery, but this is the only way he can play it.*) But he had a good life.

PAKEY. He had, half-starved. Fond of the bottle too, Mr Brown?

MR BROWN. He was, he w– Aw! No now, Patrick. Ah-haa, you were always the joker, always the –

PAKEY. Not a great sodality man, Mr Brown?

MR BROWN. Always the joker.

PAKEY. But maybe he was ashamed of his suit.

MR BROWN. Well, you never changed. (*Solemn again.*) No, Patrick, your father, Bartley Garvey, could take a drink, and he could carry it. And that was no flaw in Bartley Garvey's character.

PAKEY (*solemnly*). Musha, poor auld 'Rags'.

MR BROWN. Ah – well – yes. But you're doing well?

PAKEY. Oh, yes, Mr Brown.

MR BROWN. Saving your money, Patrick?

PAKEY. Oh yes. And when I have enough saved –

MR BROWN. You'll come home.

PAKEY. I will.

MR BROWN. And you'll be welcome.

PAKEY. And I'll buy out this town, Mr Brown.

MR BROWN. You will, sir.

PAKEY. And then I'll burn it to the ground.

MR BROWN. Hah-haa, hah-haa, joker, joker! Well now, Patrick, we're all pleased you like England and getting on well, but I'm sure you're in a hurry now, and –

PAKEY. Sure, it's a lovely country, England. And the bosses all pay great wages and –

MR BROWN. That's good – they do – that's –

PAKEY. No old hypocrites over there at all –

MR BROWN. I heard that.

PAKEY. Sure, it's a great country. Great pagan people, the English.

MR BROWN. Very nice people, we're told.

PAKEY. They mind their own business. And they don't call a man – a fool – if he's trying to enjoy himself in life.

MR BROWN. Well – well now, not many young fellas could afford the burial you gave him. And you're well able to support your mother now. We won't be delaying you, Patrick; I'm sure you have things to do. I'll just get the bill from the office. No one can say you didn't put a decent coffin on him.

MR BROWN *exits to office.*

PAKEY. I was afraid they might be talking all right.

JOHN JOE. But is it that good over there?

PAKEY. Money! To save, spend, send home, be independent, see them as they are, or whatever you want to do with it.

JOHN JOE. But –

PAKEY. But, first step, you mustn't be afraid to say – (*He makes obscene 'V' gesture.*) – to this place.

JOHN JOE. Oh, there's more to it than just that.

PAKEY. Well, if there is, it's too much for you. (*Calls as he marches into the office.*) You didn't drop dead in there yourself, did you, Mr Brown?

PAKEY *exits, marching into the office.*

MR BROWN (*off*). Oh, come in, come in, Patrick. I'm just totting up . . .

JOHN JOE. Well, if it's that good, what are you so bitter about?

JOHN JOE *takes a new packet of cigarettes from under the counter, opens them, lights one and pockets the remainder. All the time looking in the direction* PAKEY *has taken. Then he collects up the dirty cups and exits with them to rear of shop.* PAKEY *and* MR BROWN *enter.* MR BROWN *showing* PAKEY *out.*

MR BROWN. Do you remember when you used caddy for me out in the golf-links? The short little trousers on you. Did I treat you fair? Did I or didn't I always give you a tanner more than Simon Manton?

PAKEY. Like any sportsman, you liked to find your ball in a good lie always, Mr Brown.

MR BROWN. . . . Well, you're off in the morning then?

PAKEY. Were you ever in England, Mr Brown?

MR BROWN. Oh, I was. Well, it was just to touch down at London airport one time, for something or other, on our way to Lourdes.

PAKEY. Ah yes. And your piles were never cured. Look at that now! And they say faith can move mountains.

PAKEY *exits.* MR BROWN's *smile starts to fade.*

Scene Three

The kitchen. About 7.30 p.m. It is growing dark outside. FATHER is seated on the butter-box, scraping with his nails an old penny that he found in the garden. He is engrossed in what he is doing, singing snatches of a song to himself. (The song presumably is called 'The Ship That Never Returned'.) MOTHER is seated by the window, looking out. JOHN JOE is shaving in front of the mirror; shaving things and basin on the table.

MOTHER. Who's that turning the corner up there?

FATHER (*singing to himself*). 'She never returned, oh, she never returned . . .'

MOTHER. Who's that turning the corner? Look out, John Joe.

FATHER (*absently*). Wha'? (*Continues scraping and singing.*) '. . . On the ship that never returned . . . '.

MOTHER. A parcel to him. One of them tight trousers on him. He couldn't be much.

FATHER (*absently*). Wha'?

JOHN JOE. What use is it to you to know who he –

MOTHER. Aw! That'll be another parcel of clothes for Mrs Quinn back the road. That's the stuck-up lady. That's the lady that's graund. (*Accent: grand.*) And the home she came out of. That'll be where he's going now.

FATHER (*singing*). 'On the . . . ship . . . that never . . .'.

MOTHER (*suddenly, a reprimand to* JOHN JOE). Well there's no use going 'round with your eyes closed.

FATHER (*absently*). Wha'? '. . . returned . . .'.

MOTHER. More finery for the Quinns, and all knowing they have bills outstanding all over the country.

FATHER. 'Said the fair haired boy . . .'.

MOTHER. Though she always paid me regular for her washing when I used do it.

FATHER (*singing*). 'To his grey-haired mother . . .'. Wha?

MOTHER (*about to pour a cup of tea when she forgets her purpose*).
Aw! He'll be Regan, Regan! That's who he is. (*Looks out window.*)
He's gone. Regan. Coming down here fifty-two miles from
Ballinbay, working in Lardner's. Isn't it late he's delivering? Sure,
you should know him, John Joe. They have some kind of pub in
Ballinbay, but they're up to their eyes. £425 the brewery has
against him. That lad was drinking them out of house and home.
The father told him to leave. A small baldy little man. And the
brewery man was down twice to him. But an auld yoke of a
mother, doing the film star on it; and, they say, she'll be the next
to go. The old óinseach! But the father is fit for the mental home.
But they say he was an old soft auld thing always and never any
good. Peteen Mullin had it all.

FATHER (*absently*). Wha'? It's a penny I think. I found it in the
garden.

FATHER *exits to rear of house.*

(*Off; singing*) 'She never returned . . . oh, she never returned . . .'.

Pause.

MOTHER. Were ye busy today?

JOHN JOE. No.

FATHER (*off*). 'On the ship that never . . .'.

JOHN JOE. . . . Pakey Garvey came in to pay for the coffin.

MOTHER. Musha, the whole town is laughing and talking about
the same Pakey and the things he's saying.

JOHN JOE. . . . Still, he was able to pay cash for a bill of nearly
fifty pounds.

MOTHER. Oh, they say he has the money too . . . Maybe he has.

JOHN JOE. Not many young lads of his age could afford such a
funeral . . . for their . . .

MOTHER. . . . Hah?

JOHN JOE. For their parents.

MOTHER. Hah?

JOHN JOE. For his father.

MOTHER. Indeed, it's all the same to 'Rags' now what sort of cask he's buried in.

JOHN JOE. Still . . . it might be better to face the facts.

MOTHER. Hah?

JOHN JOE. I mean . . . he was talking about nicknames too.

MOTHER. Poor 'Rags'. Lord have mercy on him.

JOHN JOE. . . . They call us nicknames too.

MOTHER. They do.

Pause. MOTHER's face is now looking out window in vacant depression. JOHN JOE comes to the window to please her and to bribe her for the touch that is coming.

JOHN JOE. Look out, ma'am. There's Peteen out there.

MULLINS *has entered and is standing in the shadows, listening for a sound, glancing about him; a lonely bird in the shadows. MIKO enters on his bicycle, cycling to the town.*

MULLINS. How yeh, Miko!

MIKO (*startled*). Oh bejingoes! Well, tee-hee-hee, I caught you said the policeman! (*MIKO has exited.*)

JOHN JOE. Miko Feely.

MOTHER. Yes.

MULLINS. Where are you off to? (*MULLINS exits slowly, eyes following MIKO.*)

Short pause.

JOHN JOE. Ma'am.

MOTHER. Yes.

JOHN JOE. Ah . . . have you – few bob?

MOTHER. Hah?

JOHN JOE. Few bob.

MOTHER. Oh now, John Joe –

JOHN JOE. Could you give me six until –

MOTHER (*back in form*). Now, John Joe, there's only twenty shillings in my pound the same as anybody else's pound. (*She gets the jug without the handle from the dresser where she keeps her money.*) And the rates will coming up again in another month. And where will that come out of? And the electricity bill again today. And Peteen Mullins will be 'round in the morning for the money for his (*Father's*) insurance policy. And I'll never see a penny of that, because I'll be gone long before him. And me that's paying it and keeping it going these twelve years. You can't have money if you're spending it. I never buy anything for myself like I see other women doing. There's Peteen's wife out there and she has a new rig-out on her for every time she wants to be swanking it, and I'm the same old three-and-fourpence Sunday and Monday. He's (*Father*) bringing nothing in here except the few shillings he gets now and again for digging a grave. All some girls is out for is having a good time, and there's no use for the likes of us trying to keep up with them. And people is only laughing at them running round after girls, spending and lavishing money foolish. And as Peteen's wife abroad was saying yesterday – and I know who she was hinting at – that people before got enough of society.

JOHN JOE *has finished shaving. He starts to brush his teeth. MOTHER has counted out the six shillings, but she is not ready to hand it to him yet.*

MOTHER. I'm only giving you advice, John Joe; I'm only for your good. There's no one else cares. And not have people talking about them living above their means. There was fourteen-and-six of a bill again in Clancy's last week. I'm saying every week we'll have to cut down. But we will this week. There's too much buying of fancy soap and toothpaste and hair-oil. Believe you me, Mrs Smith doesn't. And Jack Smith is earning nine pounds a week, caretaking. Or sweet cake. That's the woman that'd make anyone wise. And the fortunes she must have stored away. (*Forgetting her purpose for a moment, she mimics MRS SMITH.*) Mmmm, crayture, darlin'. And I seen your father years ago, forever washing and scrubbing his teeth, and they all fell out in the end. (*Puts money in his hand.*) Here.

JOHN JOE. He didn't brush them the right way; up and down, not cross-ways.

MOTHER. When common soap, or salt, or bread soda, would wash them better. Or soot: I was often told that. (*She hears FATHER coming in.*) Here he's in. Put that money in your pocket now, and don't let him see it, and don't lose it, and make it last you, and be wise.

FATHER *enters, scraping the penny with a file.*

MOTHER (*looking out window*). Peteen Mullins won't let anything go unbeknownst to him. He's not asleep.

FATHER. It's a penny.

FATHER *puts the penny and the file in front of her. He sits and starts staring vacantly into the fire. After a few moments he sighs heavily. MOTHER pours a mug of tea for him and puts away the teapot. She returns to the window and looks out.*

MOTHER. That's the man (MULLINS): a top member of his Sodality and a non-drinker. (*Roughly to* FATHER.) There's a cup of tea there for you.

FATHER (*sighs; then, absently*). Wha'?

MOTHER (*harshly*). Your tea is poured out.

FATHER (*long sigh*). O-o-o-o-o, me eyes is sore!

JOHN JOE *is putting on his shirt, tie, jacket; combing his hair.*

MOTHER. Why don't you put on the striped one. (JOHN JOE *reaches for the striped shirt in exchange for the blue one.*) Or the blue one.

JOHN JOE. Hmm? Which?

MOTHER. Whichever of them you like!

A moment of indecision, a problem, for JOHN JOE. *He decides on his first choice.*

FATHER (*suddenly*). Did you get the lend of that spraying-can up town today?

MOTHER. Sure I wasn't up town, and sure you couldn't go spraying today.

FATHER (*progressively getting more vehement*). Bloody bastard, Mickeen Hayes; bloody fine spraying-can I gave him and the bastard never brought it back to me. Fine new spade I lent him too, the bastard, and he stuck to it. You – you – you couldn't get a spraying-can like it today for love or money.

MOTHER. Wasn't that twenty years ago? What was it but an old auld thing that wouldn't spray much?

FATHER (*eyes blazing*). Was it an old auld thing now? Was it? Would you get it today for ten pounds, would you? Would you? Old auld thing how-are-yeh! And Jackeen Smith abroad, didn't you give him the cartwheel I had in the yard? The rim of it I wanted to make a grate for the room in there.

MOTHER. Ary your tea is there if you want it.

FATHER. You're great! Great! . . . Great! . . . Great! (*To himself.*) Great . . . Great . . . There was no one good enough for you! . . . Great.

JOHN JOE *has finished dressing. There is a marked contrast between his appearance and theirs. He is conscious of it and feels guilty about it. He feels guilty about going out. He sits on the butter-box, hands playing with a box of cigarettes. The silence goes on.*

MOTHER. Are you going out? (*He nods.*) Well, go if you're going. But don't be staying out, letting the neighbours be seeing you coming home late like always. (*He nods his agreement.*) Hah? . . . I put in your bike.

JOHN JOE (*nods his thanks*). . . . Ah . . . (*Offering a cigarette.*) Smoke, Daddy?

FATHER. Wha'? . . . no thanks, a mac. (*Reverts to his trance.*)

MOTHER. And call in to your Uncle Alec on the way; keep in with him.

JOHN JOE (*nods*). . . . Why don't you go out for a walk or something? (MOTHER *laughs at him.*) Spring. Hah-haa!

MOTHER. What do we want out? Come here to me a minute. (*She brushes a fleck of dust off his jacket.*) Well, do you know, that's a lovely sports coat on you, John Joe!

FATHER (*coming out of trance for a moment; pleased*). Wha'? . . . 'Tis. 'Tis.

JOHN JOE (*false panache, chest out, frozen grin, swinging himself around*). Hah-haa! Hah-haa! Fine man! Fine man!

He seizes the moment, tosses the packet of cigarettes on the table and goes out the front door quickly. Once outside the front door he stops and takes a deep breath.

MULLINS. Off to meet her, John Joe?

Then he sees MULLINS has returned to his place in the shadows. Then he sees MRS SMITH and AGNES entering.

MRS SMITH. Aaaa, the boy, John Joe. Thank God now, nice night.

JOHN JOE (*smiling*). Hah-haa!

JOHN JOE exits quickly. When he is out of sight he is heard whistling.

MULLINS (*after JOHN JOE*). Hah? (*Joins MRS SMITH and AGNES; delighted with the company.*) He's in humour with the whistling, Mrs? – Off to meet his banker girl-friend, Agnes? Hah? – She's young?

MRS SMITH. Mmmmmm, banker.

MULLINS. Coming up in the world, Agnes? – Stays out late, Mrs?

MRS SMITH. Young girleens, mmm. There can be no good in it: Away from their homes. (*To AGNES.*) The pitfalleens, darlin'.

MULLINS. Hah? Oh, she does, does, out late, Mrs. Mrs Foley that has the four-shilling a week policy out with me told me. And I seen her room, and come here to me, how many – how many bottle-eens would you say she has on her table? Perfumes and lacquers and – Lagars, I call them. How many bottleens would you say in her room? How many – how many? – go on, try a guess and I'll tell ye. . . .

They are strolling off stage as the lights fade.

Scene Four

A hay shed. About midnight. JOHN JOE *and* MONA *are lying on the hay.* MONA *is singing 'I Know My Love' as the lights come up. She tries to sing it without taking a breath.*

MONA. 'I know my love by his way of walking
   And I know my love by his way of talking
   And I know my love in his suit of blue
   And if my love leaves me what will I do-oo-oo,
   And still she cried I love him the best
   And a troubled mind sure can find no re-eh-est (*rest*)
   And still she cried bonny boys are few
   And if my love leaves me what will I do?' . . . Oh, was I telling you I had a letter from mummy today.

JOHN JOE. Shhh.

MONA. Jimmy is going to the uni next autumn. My young brother. She said she was glad I had a handsome boyfriend.

JOHN JOE. What? (*Sits up.*)

MONA. That good-looking men are hard to find, she said.

JOHN JOE. You mentioned me in your letter?

MONA. Yes.

JOHN JOE. What did you say?

MONA. Well I couldn't tell her, could I, we were engaged, could I? Because you never asked me. Could I? I just said we were doing a line and that you're not too bad. Hmm? . . . No, I said you were lovely.

JOHN JOE. Did you say . . .

MONA. What?

JOHN JOE. How old I am.

MONA. Why would I mention that?

JOHN JOE. Your mother might be the same age as me.

MONA (*hurt*). That's not fair. You'd swear you were forty . . . five.

JOHN JOE (*grinning*). Aa, you're lovely too, Mona. You are, you are. I mean it.

MONA. Well, why can't you say it right besides grinning always. Haven't you seen them in the pictures, the way they say it? Daddy has a cold. Oh, do you know what he said to me the day I came working here? Mona, he said, you get a man now as handsome as your mother got.

JOHN JOE (*stands*). Hah-hah!

MONA. I'd say you'd get on well. I'd say you and daddy would –

JOHN JOE. Shhh! (*He pretends he has heard something.*) Listen! . . . I thought I heard . . .

MONA (*whispers*). What?

JOHN JOE. Someone . . . did you?

She shakes her head, listening intently. Then, suddenly, he starts to do a wild dance, sing-songing.

JOHN JOE. 'Step it out, Maggie, my fine daughter;
Step it out, Maggie, if you can;
Step it out, Maggie, my fine daughter,
And show your legs to the countryman!'
(*Then he pounces on her, shouting.*) Oh, me mother'd love you!

They roll about on the hay, laughing.

JOHN JOE (*stage-Irish brogue*). But Eileen Óg, a girleen, how would you like to leave the mists that do be on the bog and fly away to seek your fortune?

MONA. The mists that do be!

JOHN JOE. Yis! Hah? How, a girleen, would you like that?

She laughs, pulling closer to him to be kissed. They kiss. They smile at each other. JOHN JOE grows self-conscious, and, on the pretext of stretching himself, he pulls himself higher up on the hay away from her. MONA's face is worried for a moment, but she quickly dispels the thought that causes it. She smiles to herself at a new thought.

MONA. Do you know? – Are you listening? . . . You're very odd

. . . I like it though . . . And walking out miles to here always. That's where our time goes . . . I like it though . . . Do you know, you're an awful bad court? I was surprised . . . And, I'm sure, people don't really give a damn about us. And if some of them do, well it won't affect me, because I just feel sorry for them, . . . in their loneliness. (*She pulls herself up beside him.*) . . . You look nice with your eyes closed . . . What are you thinking?

JOHN JOE. Can't you be quiet?

MONA. . . . Silence is golden.

JOHN JOE. A bird in the hay is worth two in a dancehall. I wish I was rich.

MONA. That's very unusual.

JOHN JOE. If I was rich, the first thing I'd do is give a million pounds to my mother. Pay her off. No, I'm only joking . . . No. I was thinking, about – well – old people. I watch old people sometimes, and if I could be sure that they were ever fifteen or nineteen, in spite of the way things are. That-if-I-knew-that! To be able to picture her – that she ever had a moment – happy, or walking through a field. That-she-was-a-girl! . . . That I have to do something.

MONA. Yes.

JOHN JOE. Hmm?

MONA (*dispelling worry*). Away!

JOHN JOE. What? Yes. Leave. But there's something – there's *something* wrong about that.

MONA. Away! An island!

JOHN JOE. A what?

MONA. An island! A desert island!

JOHN JOE. No, the hut.

MONA. The hut?

JOHN JOE. Yis! The huteen! Up the mountings! Trees! No people –

MONA. Me! –

JOHN JOE. Straw on the floor! Nice smell! Room to stretch! And the only light would be light from the fire. No turf though, no coal, none of that. Log fire.

MONA. And a dog.

JOHN JOE. No dog.

MONA. Aw but –

JOHN JOE. Have to feed him –

MONA. Aw but –

JOHN JOE. Clean out after him. No dog, no couch, none of that. One stool.

MONA. What for?

JOHN JOE. For the cat. And when not in use, for yourself to sit on, with arms akimbo.

MONA. What?

JOHN JOE. The name of the cat: Akimbo. And the hut would be made of timber. . . . Hmm?

MONA. It's lovely.

JOHN JOE. Well, would you like to go there?

MONA. Would you bring me?

JOHN JOE. Amn't I after asking you. (*Short pause.*) I'm thinking of . . .

MONA. . . . England? (*He looks puzzled for a moment, then nods.*) When?

JOHN JOE. Soon, I think.

MONA. I'm ready.

JOHN JOE. I'll give you a shout.

MONA. . . . I'd love to . . . but I never really know . . . what you think of me. (*Shyly.*) You know . . . I know I say silly things. And I wonder why I say them. But they don't matter. Because it's what I feel . . . And I understand.

JOHN JOE. . . . Well, I . . . frankly . . . I think you're great.

MONA (*studies his face for a moment. Then she smiles*). . . . Enough said.

They smile at each other for a moment.

MONA. Look at the time. -

JOHN JOE. We'd better go.

They exit. Off, MONA sings – this time slowly:

MONA. 'I know my love is an arrant rover,
I know my love roams the wild world over,
In some foreign port he will chance to tarry,
And don't you know he will surely marry,
And still she cried, I love him the best,
And a troubled mind sure can find no rest,
And still she cried, bonny boys are few,
And if my loves leaves me what will I do?'

Scene Five

Tuesday

A spot of unreal (but beautiful) light on JOHN JOE, who is sitting up in bed, arms akimbo, delighted in this dream of his new address. He sits, not daring to move anything but his eyes, in case a movement should dispel the new surroundings. The speech is whispered, urgent, swift, rhythmic, without pause, as if unpunctuated; a delighted racing mind.

JOHN JOE. And how are you now, John Joe? Very well thank you. And how do you like England? Very well thank you. But it's America. Very well thank you. Your address? – What? Your address – Oh! Your address – Yes. Two-two-two A, Tottenham Court Road, Madison Square Gardens, Lower Edgebaston, Upper Fifth Avenue, Camden Town, U.S.A., S.W.6. And it's very nice over here. I made it! – I made it! No pot lately shined calls the kettle black. Everyone's pink like the image of God. My room – My address – Well, look at it – look at it! The walls, white walls, not cluttered, but Spring; no trespassers jarring the trembling.

Look at those fields, the first soft grass! Look at the bracken, the smell of the bog, and Gardenfield Wood whispering to Molloy! I made it! – I got here! Sure Pakey Garvey isn't free at all. Or Frank, poor Frank. But there's no flies on me. And no bitterness, mind. And they're all right at home. No, they didn't have to die! She told me she smelt the primroses once, a print dress and her hair, walking Cloonasscragh. God bless you, I said. Say it again. God bless them, I say, and was free with a smile, obviously right for emigration. I got here, I got here! See that box over there? Treasure, gold. Big box – the big box – bigger box – the biggest one! To be sent home to Mammy, cause now I'm of use. And, oh, there's nothing futile about you, John Joe. No-no, but sensible, practical, reasonable, logical. And I shall have some peace here. Breathe in. (*He starts to inhale. There's a knock at the door. He gasps, alarmed.*) Ah! (*But almost immediately his delight returns.*) Aaaa! That will be Monda, Mona, Mo-o-na, making a nice, clean, civilized and useful visit. (*Second knock at the door; he smiles.*) I always let my wife knock three times to prove the point of my privacy. I'm very happy now.

He relaxes his arms, closes his eyes, smiles, awaiting the third knock. The lighting changes to normal morning light. The church clock is ringing nine. It is Tuesday morning. MOTHER, 'distracted' is pushing bicycle through the kitchen. A large pile of clothes on the kitchen table waiting to be ironed.

MOTHER. The state he has me in here every morning! Lord, isn't it terrible? How many times have I called him? It's gone nine! You're late – late – late for work! Late for work Monday, later for work Tuesday! That's the good the high-ups is doing him! (*She is pushing the bicycle out the front door.*) Peteen Mullins has his water drawn these fifteen minutes. (*Checks the pressure in the tyres.*) Aw, Lord! (*Rushing back to kitchen; searching for bicycle pump.*) Where's the pump? Where's the pump? Where, in cursed hell is the pump? The bike is flat, the bike is flat! And me that'll suffer at the end of the week trying to make ends meet.

JOHN JOE *is now sitting up in bed, eyes open, feeling the loss of his new address. He is about to get out of bed when she enters his room. MOTHER is carrying the bicycle pump and his shoes. She throws down the shoes.*

MOTHER. Are you getting up at all today? . . . All right, stay there, John Joe; stay there then. Don't get up, sleep on. That's the way. I'm up since half-past six ironing and mending for the town, but you stay there now. That's the right thing to do, that's what everyone else is doing. Don't go to work.

VOICE (*off, on road*). Are ye in trouble?

And MULLINS *enters, a note book and pencil in his hand, approaching Moran's.* MOTHER *goes to kitchen for insurance book and money.*

JOHN JOE (*to himself*). Yis-yis-yis, we'll have snow, mmmm, right, I won't go to work!

He pulls the bed-clothes over his head. MOTHER *comes out to* MULLINS *who is at the front door and gives him money and insurance book. She starts to pump bicycle.* MULLINS *makes an entry in both books.*

MULLINS. Hah? . . . Hah? . . . Here, Mrs Moran, let me do that. (*He pumps the bicycle for her.*) Hah? . . . He's late? Air going in? Is he going to work? Not punctured anyway. Hah? Twenty minutes late now, sure?

MOTHER. The one morning won't matter.

MULLINS. It's pumped. Jobs are scarce, Mrs? Isn't he the diveleen too? Look at that mudguard. And how long has he that bike? Last November twelve months isn't it he got it? Sixteen – seventeen months, is it? I knew that.

MRS SMITH *and* AGNES *enter. They are carrying some parcels.* AGNES *unashamedly chewing sweets.*

MRS SMITH. Thank God now, thank the good God, a lovely morning!

MULLINS (*watching parcels*). Hah?

MRS SMITH. We didn't meet John Joe, the boy, aaaa!

MOTHER. A touch of a throat.

MULLINS. Hah?

MOTHER. The tonsils.

MRS SMITH. Crayture. Sore thingeens. Run for the red flannelette the Rosary Priest himself blessed, Agnes, darlin'.

MULLINS (*shaking the bicycle*). And the mudguard, Mrs?

MOTHER. It's nothing; just a touch.

MRS SMITH. Aaaa, the bike-een. And there's a yoke under the dresser –

MOTHER. Sure it's all right.

MRS SMITH. It'll tighten it for him, darlin'

MULLINS. I've scores of wrenches at home myself. I'll do it for him, Mrs?

MOTHER. No, thanks.

MRS SMITH. Run, Agnes.

MOTHER. No thanks, Agnes.

MULLINS. Cause I can do it before I continue my rounds.

MOTHER. No.

MRS SMITH. Sure now, a graw?

MULLINS. Are you sure, Mrs?

MOTHER. He's planning to do a big job on it himself. Thanks, thank ye now.

MOTHER *goes to kitchen.*

MRS SMITH (*exiting*). Cause if we can't succour one another Mmmmmmmm!

MULLINS, MRS SMITH *and* AGNES *exit.*

MOTHER. . . . Not a one here to put a drop of oil on that auld jiggler of a bike. The whole town laughing at us. Leaving it out in hail, rain and snow. That's the house we have! Not a one to do a blessed thing unless I do it myself. (*Then, grandly.*) Well, others can relax too!

She sits stiff-backed, craning her neck, on the butterbox. After a moment the pose collapses, face softening, into hopelessness, into memories, staring into the fire. ALEC *enters, coming from his shop; he comes into the kitchen.*

ALEC (*hearty*). How yeh, Julia! How are you getting it? I had a great longing all day yesterday for a taste of a nice young head of cauliflower. But I got into such a humour about eleven o'clock that I wouldn't please myself to come out and ask you for one. Cabbage and lettuce for the colour; there's nothing like it for the roses in your cheeks.

MOTHER (*answering absently*). The cabbage out there is too small yet. One of them wouldn't make a dinner for anyone.

ALEC. Well, wouldn't two of them!

MOTHER (*rises; she starts the ironing; she shakes off the depression, her old form returning*). There isn't a lot out in that garden, of cabbage or lettuce or anything.

ALEC (*punning*). Ary, let us alone, she said. (*He pours himself a cup of tea.*)

MOTHER. How could there, sure? No one to mind the piece of a garden right. But I'm telling you, the good times are finished and done with.

ALEC. They were done with a long time ago, Julia.

MOTHER. Persons high-skyting round the country, while the fools keep slaving.

ALEC. You work too hard, Julia, and the world is giving you no thanks for it.

MOTHER. But if the money isn't coming in –

ALEC. It can't go out: you're right, on me oath you are.

MOTHER. If we were like some of the people going, with the dip-in-the-dip and leave the herring for father, we'd be better off, besides gloffering ourselves up with food.

ALEC. Aa, that auld wiristhru of a bitch Mrs Smith is too miserly altogether; I don't like her, religious or not.

MOTHER. And there's too much supplying of this-that-and-the-other from the garden.

ALEC (*moves towards rear of house*). Well, I'll – Is Tom out there? – I'll just –

MOTHER *shakes her head and motions him to sit; that her anger is not for him; she nods her head at* JOHN JOE's *room.*

MOTHER (*loudly*). But maybe he's becoming like his brother! Maybe we're getting on his nerves here! Maybe he wants a holiday! Maybe he's thinking of going off, leaving! Maybe he's – (*She stops short; instinct has been working. She becomes frightened at the thought.*) . . . But he knows better, I'm telling you. with his soft times here. People waiting hand and foot on him. (*She starts to cry.*) . . . Why won't he get up?

ALEC. What's on yeh, Julia?

MOTHER (*dries her tears*). . . . How's the shop, Alec?

ALEC. How's the – ? It's well!

MOTHER (*fiercely*). Well, he's the nearest one to you; he's your nephew!

ALEC. I'm not dead yet!

MOTHER (*starts to cry again – or feigning tears*). Go in, Alec, and talk to him. See is he going in to work the half day itself.

She pours a cup of tea for ALEC *to take in to* JOHN JOE. ALEC *goes to* JOHN JOE's *room.*

ALEC (*loudly*). What's on you, you whore you! Will you get up! You're like the Aggie Khannie there in bed! (*He winks at* JOHN JOE *and closes the door.*) Here's a cup of tea for you. Oh Jasus, me feet are killing me! (*He sits.*) What was I saying? Varicose veins. They'll go to me head if I'm not careful. (*He laughs.*) That's what I said to the doctor. He said I needed a support, a cane, he said. But would I hell give the neighbours the satisfaction of seeing me with a stick. What was I saying? Oh yes, Was I telling you I'll be drawing my first week's old-age pension in ten days' time? I'll be on top of the wheel. . . . Well, you're in awful humour. Is it the girls that's troubling you? Did your girl friend throw up up?

JOHN JOE. Yeh.

ALEC. You mustn't be any use to her. You have to keep knocking an odd old tumble out of them.

JOHN JOE. Do you think?

ALEC. And isn't that what they – Oh, you whore you!

They laugh. JOHN JOE *sips his tea.*

JOHN JOE. I'm going to England, Alec.

ALEC. Yes?

JOHN JOE. . . . Well, what do you think?

ALEC. Sure that's not for me to think. Sure, I never thought, and it's not the time for me to go starting now.

MR BROWN *has entered and is knocking at the front door.* JOHN JOE *and* ALEC *listen.* MOTHER *leaves her ironing to answer the door.* MR BROWN *is angry.*

MR BROWN. Good morning.

MOTHER. Oh!

MR BROWN. Is John in?

MOTHER. Oh, he –

MR BROWN. Will you ask him has he the keys to my store-room?

MOTHER. I'll – yes. He's in bed, sir; the throat, tonsils, Mr Brown.

MR BROWN. If he's sick, he's sick.

MOTHER. Oh, he is, Mr Brown.

MR BROWN. But I have a business to run. If I'm employing him I'm employing him.

MOTHER. Yes, sir, yes?

MR BROWN. A customer standing there now. And I can't tolerate –

MOTHER. Oh dear – customer – business to run, Mr Brown?

MR BROWN. It's hard to run a business if, you know –

MOTHER. Yes, yes, yes, sir –

MR BROWN. In one day, out the next.

MOTHER. Yes, yes –

MR BROWN. You understand.

MOTHER. Oh yes, indeed, sir.

MR BROWN. Punctuality.

MOTHER. Certainly. (*She sees she is softening him.*)

MR BROWN. And my staff –

MOTHER. Staff.

MR BROWN. I've always had the tradition among my –

MOTHER. Staff –

MR BROWN. Employees –

MOTHER. Employees –

MR BROWN. To join certain societies.

MOTHER. That's right, Mr Brown.

MR BROWN. I'm not saying John Joe isn't a good lat but –

MOTHER. Societies, Mr Brown?

MR BROWN. You see, an employer's obligations towards his employees, Mrs Moran. To mould them, if you follow me. After all, if we are what we're supposed to be, Catholic country. And if only the other employers in the town would take their spiritual obligations the same way. But I'm on to them too.

MOTHER. Sure, everyone knows all you do, Mr Brown. And you'll have your reward so you will. Where would we be at all without the religion?

MR BROWN (*has now settled down to chat*). You see, Mrs Moran, take up the newspaper any day of the week, and what does it say? What will you see there, as plain as the nose on your face, in capital letters of black and white? You will find it says what? You will find it says 'Times Are Changing'. The world is upset, sir. It was only last night I was saying to Mrs Brown in bed: The universe is trembling, I said to her. There's wars and councils and new fangled notions all about us. They're trying out untried ideas. Now what should be our role in this unstable comuffle of affairs? She said nothing but she thought about it. Our role, I said, is to be the anchor. We can be and will be the anchor of this trembling universe. We'll stick to the guns God gave us, and when they are through with their points of order and points of disorder we'll still be the same, a shining anchor up there in the sky for them. Times are changing, but the money isn't circulating. Ah-haa, you understand what I'm saying now! And it's the reverse of that we want. The reverse of that is our ideal, sir. There are men like myself, Mrs Moran, paying out high wages, and we have all sorts of –

On the word 'wages' JOHN JOE *comes out of his room pulling up his pants.*

JOHN JOE. £98 a week, Mr Brown!

MOTHER. John Joe!

MR BROWN *is taken off guard.*

JOHN JOE. What staff are you talking about? Myself and the messenger-boy you get in for the weekends?

MOTHER. John Joe!

JOHN JOE. I'll join the Sodality or Legion of Mary of my own free will if I want to.

MOTHER. John Joe!

JOHN JOE. It's a well-known fact you came into this town a stranger, without a shoe on your foot, but you came up fast.

MR BROWN. I – I know what people are saying about me.

JOHN JOE. And it wasn't long before you owned your employer's shop.

MR BROWN. I was left – I was left –

JOHN JOE. And he was broke –

MR BROWN. My uncle in America died –

JOHN JOE. What right have you to –

MR BROWN. I was left fourteen hundred and –

JOHN JOE. To be preaching to anyone? –

MR BROWN. Fourteen hundred pounds he left me! And – (*He stops, realizing what is happening.*) Aw, listen here now!

JOHN JOE. No. You listen here.

MR BROWN. A customer waiting!

JOHN JOE. No, you listen here –

MR BROWN. I don't have to stand here listening to your –

JOHN JOE. What are you standing there for then? –

MR BROWN. My keys!

JOHN JOE. What are you standing here for then? (*He has been rooting in his pockets for the keys. He produces them.*)

MR BROWN (*snaps keys*). Your job –

JOHN JOE. Jesus job! I can earn seven ten a week anywhere in 1958!

MR BROWN. You're only – you're only – you're only a dreamer!

He exits.

JOHN JOE (*stopped by the last remark for a moment; then*). Malachy! And stick your job and your bags of rotten onions and your sugar and your stringy sausages!

FATHER *and* ALEC *are inside front door at this stage.* MOTHER *is crestfallen.* JOHN JOE *is feeling something of an elation. He looks at each of them in turn, almost fiercely and marches into his room where he starts to dress.* MOTHER, FATHER *and* ALEC *are silent for a few moments. They go to the kitchen in single file.* MOTHER *sits on the butter box, rocking herself backwards and forwards.* FATHER *feels sorry for her.*

MOTHER (*whispering*). Now he's lost his job! Now he's lost his job!

FATHER. Tck-tck-tck-tck-tck!

MOTHER. I knew it! I knew it!

FATHER. Tck-tck-tck-tck-tck!

MOTHER. Lord above, sweet Jesus Mary, Holy Mother of God!

ALEC. Ary do you think –

MOTHER. Jesus, isn't it shocking!

FATHER. Tck-tck!

ALEC. Ary, do you think that whore Brown is all the holiness he puts on, no more than the others?

MOTHER. Oh, stop, Alec.

FATHER. Stop!

ALEC. True for John Joe –

MOTHER. The whole town will know. And the priest.

ALEC. Ary, what?

MOTHER. Fr. Daly will say we're a nice crowd.

FATHER. Fr. Daly, tck!

MOTHER. And Fr. Daly getting him the job.

ALEC. Isn't he only one man?

FATHER. Tck!

MOTHER. Oh, stop, Alec. (*Whispering at* JOHN JOE's *room.*) Are you satisfied now.

FATHER. Are you satisfied now?

MOTHER. You should be, you amadán yeh!

FATHER (*shouting*). Watch yourself now!

ALEC. Ary, Tom.

FATHER (*shouting*). I'm telling you now! So I am!

MOTHER. Oh, stop, stop, stop, stop, stop.

FATHER (*shouting*). Watch yourself now! . . .

MOTHER. Stop.

FATHER (*roaring*). So I am!

MOTHER (*harshly*). Stop, will you!

MOTHER looks at ALEC as he becomes part of some plan she is making.

ALEC. What is it Julia?

MOTHER (*gets her hat and coat*). The cabbage won't be right for another couple of weeks, but the scallions is nice, and anything else you'd like.

ALEC. Where are you off to, Julia?

MOTHER. Where do you think? I'm going down to Fr. Daly before someone else brings him the news. (*Going out the door.*) Jesus, Mary and Joseph, isn't it terrible!

MOTHER exits.

FATHER (*exiting to rear of house*). Tck-tck-tck-tck-tck!

ALEC exits, following FATHER. JOHN JOE is fully dressed in his room examining the hold-all. He puts the hold-all on the floor.

JOHN JOE. No, it's too small.

He comes out of the house and stands outside the front door. MIKO enters on bicycle. He wears a shop-assistant's coat. He has a parcel on the bike. MIKO is about forty-five; a drinker; a nervous habit of giggling, tee-hee-hee, and rubbing his hands together.

MIKO. Hello dare (*there*) Swannee River, he said!

JOHN JOE. Miko!

MIKO. I just seen your boss fuming up the road. Not a salute from him. Point of information: what can be the matter at all, boys, I said to myself, and all this lovely Spring sunshine about? And I came to the conclusion, tee-hee-hee: begobs, says I to myself, the haemorrhoids must be in a state of turmoil. Well, tee-hee-hee!

JOHN JOE. What are you doing out?

MIKO. I'm delivering lingerie, that's what I'm doing! The little fart of a messenger-boy is out sick again. The flu, bejingoes! And I'm missing my tea, delivering six pairs of knickers and a double-lined raincoat to Miss Agnes Smith. What can she want them for, tee-hee-hee, I said to myself? Or can her luck have changed?

JOHN JOE. I told him to stick it.

MIKO. Can this be her trousseau, I said to – You didn't?

JOHN JOE. I did.

MIKO. Well, you didn't?

JOHN JOE. I did. Jesus, I said, I can earn seven ten a week anywhere in 1958.

MIKO. What? Well, fair play to you! Face the ball, Carrantrylla? I always knew you were that sort of man. Lock her, Basil, or she'll dike yeh! . . . England for you now, John Joe?

JOHN JOE (*puzzled for a moment at the repetitiveness of this suggestion.*) Yeh. London.

MIKO. Well, London Town! A touch of the wild colonial boys, bejingoes!

JOHN JOE. A suitcase is all I need now.

MIKO. A nice little portmanteau.

JOHN JOE. How much are the suitcases in your place, Miko?

MIKO. What? Sure, they're from nineteen and elevenpence. But, sure, you don't want to go buying one. I've an old one at home, tee-hee-hee, if you know what I mean. (*He winks at* JOHN JOE, *rubbing his hands together.* JOHN JOE *winks, understanding.*) Up she flew, he said, and the cock kicked her! You'd do me a turn yourself. I'll slip one out of the store for you, but I won't get a chance till tomorrow. And I'll leave it in to Mary in Gavins' pub.

JOHN JOE. Sound, Miko. You won't forget?

MIKO. No. Here, I'd better be delivering these articles to the quare one. Well, you're an awful man! But I always knew it. (*Pushing off on bicycle.*) She's far from the land, he said, but she can't swim a stroke! Do you think will she give me the tea? An awful man! Well, ho-ho Chi Minh!

MIKO *exits.* JOHN JOE *goes into his room. Restless, excited, giggling. He kicks the hold-all under the bed, throws himself on the bed, kicking his feet in the air. The lights fade.*

Scene Six

Wednesday

The kitchen. Wednesday afternoon. FR. DALY *and* JOHN JOE *sit, one at each side of the table.* FR. DALY *is about fifty-five; well-meaning; a shrewd provincial administrator; a smiling face that invites one to talk. After a conversation with him one wonders if one has said too much.* JOHN JOE *is on guard.*

FR. DALY. Well, is that so? Well, confidentially – I might as well tell you – I never had much interest in football myself either. But listen to me, I'd preach ten sermons at the Women's Sodality to go to a coursing meeting. Thank God, John Joe, for the greyhounds. (*Laughs.*) Yes, aw yes. And you left Mr Brown?

JOHN JOE. I – well – I did, yes, Father.

FR. DALY. Aw yes. He has lot of customers, hasn't he?

JOHN JOE. Ah – he has, yes. Towards the end of the week.

FR. DALY. Yes . . . Hmm? . . . He can be a bit exacting – demanding to work for, John Joe?

JOHN JOE. Yes – he can be a bit – yes – that way.

FR. DALY. Though a decent man. A decent man. He takes a great interest in the town. Great. (*He laughs.*) There was a boy working for him one time and he couldn't agree with Mr Brown at all. But, one day, he threw his apron at poor Mr Brown, and he wasn't two hands higher than a duck. But, said the little lad to him, 'I'd put my fist through yeh'. (*Laughing heartily.*) A little lad, that size. Yes, aw yes. And is he hard to work for, John Joe?

JOHN JOE. Well, he's not the easiest. And he expects you to . . . He's not the easiest.

FR. DALY. Well, is he like that? . . . What age are now, John Joe?

JOHN JOE. I'm nearly thirty-four, Father.

FR. DALY. Well, are you? Well, are you? Well, I never thought that now. Ah-haaa, we'll soon have to get you married hmm? . . . But maybe you're looking after that side of things yourself, wha'? . . . I hear you have a nice young girl, John Joe? . . . What age is she?

JOHN JOE. Ah – I'm – I'm not sure, Father.

FR. DALY. Is she twenty-one?

JOHN JOE. Oh, she is easily, Father.

FR. DALY. Is she thirty?

JOHN JOE. God, I'd say she is, Father!

FR. DALY. Aw, I wouldn't say she is now, wha'? . . . She's a bank girl, isn't she?

JOHN JOE. She is, Father.

FR. DALY. Well, aren't you the little tootler! . . . She mustn't be long left school?

JOHN JOE. Ah – No – I don't think so, Father.

FR. DALY (pause; thinking; grave face). No . . . A young girl . . . But I'm sure she's a good girl . . . Yes. Very young. (He looks up; smiling again.) Well, I happened to bump into your mother yesterday. Decent woman. Hardworking woman. And . . . I'm thinking Mr Manton might need a good man in his place. What day is today?

JOHN JOE. Wednesday, Father.

FR. DALY. Wednesday. I have some business to see him about in a day or two, and . . . Yes, aw yes, I'm sure we can fix-up something. Oh, before I forget it, there's nothing bothering you, is there, that you'd like to talk over with me?

JOHN JOE. No, Father.

FR. DALY. That's good, good man, that's good . . . Sometimes, young men . . . Well, without mentioning any names now, there's a certain man in this town, and I remember well – indeed, I do – having a chat with him one time. And what's this he said to me now? Oh yes. 'This town', he said, 'is like a graveyard with walking pus-eaten corpses, and fat maggots jumping from one corpse to the next, looking for newses.' (*He laughs heartily, inviting* JOHN JOE *to join him.*) Wasn't it a good one? 'No rhyme or reason to anything in the town.' He said it straight out to me. Aw yes. That was about – what? Ten? – twelve years ago. And when I meet him now, I always remind him of it. And do you know what he says to me? 'I had no sense of humour in them days, Father.' But, I said to him that day had he honestly tried to understand the place – his parents too. 'Wasn't I born here?' he said. But, as you know, and as I told him, that isn't enough. A person kicks against something – maybe one solitary thing they find wrong. And then they set up barriers against everything else. Young people, John Joe. 'Well', I said to this man, 'you'll promise me now you'll try again.' 'But I tried', he said. 'You'll try again', I said. 'And an honest try this time, mind. Just once more.' 'Look around you', I said, 'for the good things. Open up your vision. You're a young man', I said, 'and you'll know all about it in a few years' time. And', I said, 'have – a – sense – of – humour.' Aw, the sense of humour is a great thing! That man is earning anything up to eleven pounds a week now. I know that for a fact. And he's very good to his mother. A dutiful son. He got married – when was it? – about three years ago. A nice girl. A good sensible girl. And yes if I'm not mistaken, she was something in the dressmaking line. Something like that. Aw, but I'm telling you too much. Oh, there's a lot of things you'd never think of can upset a man's life. Wha'? . . . But, 'graveyard with . . .' Wasn't it a good one?

JOHN JOE. 'Twas, Father.

FR. DALY. You'd be surprised now if I told you who that man was, but I won't tell you. All a person has to do is try. God knows there are plenty of things wrong here, but I wouldn't exchange those trifles for the hoard of evil that exists in the outside world. Don't you agree?

JOHN JOE. Yes, Father.

FR. DALY. Of course, of course. And do you think you understand the town?

JOHN JOE. Ah . . .

FR. DALY. Hmm?

JOHN JOE. No, I don't think so, Father.

FR. DALY (*surprise*). Oh?

JOHN JOE. Sometimes I think everyone is mad!

FR. DALY (*laughs*). Sense of humour, John Joe. See the good side of things. All you have to do is try.

JOHN JOE. But I tr –

FR. DALY. Ah-haa! Do you see what I mean? Isn't that what the other man said to me? Isn't it? Hmm?

JOHN JOE. 'Tis, Father.

FR. DALY. Once more now, an honest try, will you?

JOHN JOE. . . . I will, Father.

FR. DALY. Good man, John Joe; that's the spirit. Maybe now, if you want to, you'd like to take the Pledge. It'd be a great start.

JOHN JOE. No, Father, I know I wouldn't keep it.

FR. DALY. All right, John Joe. Not another word about it. I've great faith in your word for refusing, when you think you're not ready for it yet. (*Glances at his watch.*) Well, there's nothing else bothering you then?

JOHN JOE. . . . Well, there's . . .

FR. DALY. Yes?

JOHN JOE. It's . . . It's a bit silly. Nothing.

FR. DALY (*glances at watch again*). Hmm?

JOHN JOE. Well, lately . . . Something that's on my mind about . . . Well a cat has kittens, and, after a time, the kittens leave, well, home. To seek better conditions and . . . Well, the kittens, if they stay, well, they get between the mother and father, and maybe become opponents of the parents. And, well, we're all – we're all animals and (FR. DALY *is smiling.*) . . . Ah, it's a bit silly.

FR. DALY. Hmm? . . . Tck-tck-tck! Leave the cats to the women, John Joe, and get a dog for yourself. Man is made in the likeness of God, not in the likeness of your kittens. A nice little pup out of 'Tolka Row II'. (*They go to the front door.*) Nothing else then? – Good man. And I'll see Mr Manton about that job. Oh, weren't you just going out when I arrived?

JOHN JOE. I was only going up town to collect . . . (*the suitcase.*)

FR. DALY. Well, we can be walking up together.

JOHN JOE. It can wait.

FR. DALY. Well, you'll remember your promise?

JOHN JOE. I will.

FR. DALY. Good man. God bless you now.

> FR. DALY *exits. The lights fade to evening light.* JOHN JOE *remains at the door, motionless, during the change.* MULLINS *enters and stands in his place in the shadows; a lonely figure. He sees* JOHN JOE.

MULLINS. How yeh, John Joe! Hah?

JOHN JOE. Peter. (*About to go into the house; decides to 'try' again. He goes to* MULLINS.) Nice evening, Peter.

MULLINS. Hah? 'Tis. You had Fr. Daly in to you today. Nice little man? – Shrewd little man? – Fond of money too? Long time since he used be out after us one time in the wood with a flashlamp. He had a stick in them days. Will the weather keep up? (*At the sky.*) Hah-hah-hah? I've a lockeen of last year's turf still in the bog. Thought I'd shift it home on Friday.

JOHN JOE. Do you want a hand?

MULLINS. Hah? Oh, that'd be great. Did you hear about all the clothes and the parcels the Smiths is buying? They're saying Agnes is getting married. Hah? You didn't hear anything, did you? Hah? . . .

> *The light has faded to night.* JOHN JOE *and* MULLINS *have exited through the above, strolling down the road.*

Scene Seven

Thursday

Before and as the lights come up FATHER, *off, in the garden, is heard singing:*

> I am bidding farewell to the land of my youth
> And the home that I love so well;
> The mountains grand of my own native land
> I am bidding them all farewell;
> With an aching heart I will bid them adieu,
> For tomorrow I'm sailing away,
> To seek a home o'er the raging foam,
> On the shores of Americae.

The church clock is ringing eleven. MOTHER *has several bags of washing around her in the kitchen; she places the chairs in readiness for the bath.* JOHN JOE *comes from the bedroom.*

MOTHER. You had a good sleep last night. I didn't hear you tossing and turning. (*He nods, smiles and exits to get the bath for her.*) Don't go dirtying yourself with that – (*He returns with bath and places it on the chairs; he takes two buckets from the bath and moves towards front door.*) Don't go splashing your clothes, John Joe.

He comes out of house to draw the water from the pump. MRS SMITH *and* AGNES, *each with a bucket, are also converging on the pump. And* ALEC *is sitting outside his shop luxuriating in the sun.*

MRS SMITH. The patron saint of travellers, St. Christopher, St. Christopher, darlin'.

JOHN JOE *joins them.*

JOHN JOE. Morning.

MRS SMITH. Aaaa, the boy, John Joe. But a prayer to the Blessed Virgin is worth twenty to any of the others. Hasn't she the right ear of God? (JOHN JOE *nods.*) Isn't she his own mother? (AGNES *nods.* MRS SMITH's *bucket is filled. Leaving them.*) Crayture-eens!

ALEC (*calls*). Mrs Smith! Mrs Smith! Isn't it an awful dangerous thing to be doing?

MRS SMITH. What, Alec?

ALEC. Scratching your backside with a broken bottle.

MRS SMITH (*failing to make it sound like a laugh*). Mmmmmm.

She exits.

ALEC. Well, do you know, Agnes, your mother is getting more spritely every day. It must be the religion. Carelessly elegant is what she is. But sure ye were the good-looking family too. (AGNES *is moving off with her bucket.*) And yourself, Agnes. On me oath! Fine and plump – isn't she, John Joe? – God bless her. (*Whispers to* JOHN JOE.) Kiss me arse.

AGNES (*turns back, just before exiting; faintest trace of a smile*). A prayer to St. Jude for you, Alec.

ALEC. St. Who? (AGNES *exits.*) St. Who, did she say? St. Jude? Isn't he the man in charge of hopeless cases? (JOHN JOE *laughs.* ALEC *laughs. Then, appreciating* AGNES.) Now! And I always thought that girl was only a ludhramaun. (*He looks up, admiring the sky.*) Aa, He didn't make too many mistakes at all.

JOHN JOE *takes the bucket of water into the kitchen.* MOTHER *starts to wash clothes. Off,* FATHER *is singing.* MOTHER *pauses to wipe her brow.*

MOTHER. Why don't you go out and sit in the sun for yourself. (JOHN JOE *moves towards front door.*) Leave Alec alone today. (JOHN JOE *looks enquiringly at her.*) Not to be sitting out there: Strangers passing, wondering why you're not at work.

JOHN JOE (*exiting rear of house*). I'll go out and see what Daddy is doing.

MOTHER. Don't go dirtying yourself! Don't go – (*To herself as she resumes work.*) Don't go.

A MAN with a briefcase enters on the road outside. He sees the signboard over ALEC's *window. He approaches* ALEC.

MAN. Good day!

ALEC. Good day, sir!

MAN. Would you be Alec Brady?

ALEC. I am.

MAN. Alec Francis Brady?

ALEC. . . . Who am I speaking to now?

MAN. Oh, I'm a pension officer. (*He opens his briefcase.*) You're a very young-looking pensioner.

ALEC. Oh, me daddy dad the nice shape on his jaws no more than myself.

MAN (*laughs; takes out a document*). Are you sure there isn't another Alec Francis Brady?

ALEC. Well, there could be, sir. Me daddy, along with having the nice jaws, was a randy auld night-skyter.

MAN (*laughs*). Well, we have a report about you here.

ALEC (*smiling*). A what, a report, yes?

MAN. Is this your shop?

ALEC. It is. Woolworks!

MAN. But you made no mention of it in your application for the pension.

ALEC (*smile has faded*). Wha'?

MAN. It's a question of the means test. You didn't declare this source of income.

ALEC. I – I – (*Trying to joke.*) Me daddy's – me daddy's memory, no more than me own, was . . . (*His world has collapsed.*) . . . What will it mean?

The pension officer looks in through the shop window.

MAN. We shall have to look into the matter, of course. But I'd imagine that despite the shop you will qualify.

ALEC (*absently*). What?

MAN. Perhaps we could go inside and fill up this new form.

ALEC (*absently*). The shop was only company to me.

MAN. This new application form.

ALEC. The shop is making nothing, that's why I didn't enter it.

MAN. I can see for myself it's only a detail, but –

ALEC. Who told on me?

MAN. Oh, I can't – Nobody, I'm sure.

ALEC (*angry*). Who wrote in then about me?

MAN. Only a detail, but rather than having too much delay in your receiving the thing –

ALEC. Mullins, was it?

MAN. It would be better –

ALEC. Who knows everybody's business –

MAN. To straighten it out now.

ALEC. Oh, the whore! The get! The informer's breed!

MAN. Let's go inside, Mr Brady, and fill up this . . .

Pension officer exits to shop. ALEC *follows him.*

ALEC (*off*). It was Mullins, wasn't it? Mullins! Amn't I right? Amn't I right?

In the kitchen MOTHER *has stopped to listen to* ALEC's *shouting – but only for a moment; then she resumes working more doggedly than ever.* FATHER, *with excited curiosity, enters from garden carrying a spade.*

FATHER. Who's Alec shouting at?

MOTHER. Did you sow them potatoes?

FATHER (*looking out window*). Wha' – wha'? – wha'?

MOTHER. Come-away-from-the-windy! (*The severity of her command surprises him.*) . . . A new job won't stop him leaving.

FATHER exits to rear of house. The pension man enters, coming from ALEC's *house, and exits. The light is fading to evening light. Off, in the garden,* FATHER *has resumed singing:*

FATHER (*off*). . . .
It's not for the greed of gold that I go

O'er the stormy and raging sea,
But to seek a home for my own true love
On the shores of Americae.

ALEC *enters and sits outside his shop. He has been drinking; he carries the empty bottle. Despite his outburst later in the scene, he is now a tired old man, the jauntiness is gone.* MOTHER *has almost completed her day's washing.* JOHN JOE *comes into kitchen from the garden.*

JOHN JOE. What was all the rumpus about out there earlier?

MOTHER. Go out to Alec. Talk nice to him. Comfort him.

JOHN JOE. What happened?

MOTHER. How do I know what happened? (*Harshly.*) A stranger called. Did ever a stranger bring us good news? (*Gently; leads him to the door.*) Go on.

JOHN JOE *goes out to* ALEC. MOTHER *stands outside front door, but she does not join them.*

JOHN JOE. Well, Alec! . . . What is it?

ALEC. . . . Oh, he said there'd likely be a delay. But I'd get it . . . But the good is knocked out of it for me now. They have me crawling at last. (*He puts the bottle on the ground.*) I bet you don't know where they're making poteen, right under the guards' noses in the middle of the town? . . . The pension man was here. The means tests. I didn't declare the shop.

MOTHER *goes into the kitchen. She exits to rear of house with the washing.*

JOHN JOE. What?

ALEC. I'm waiting for Mullins.

JOHN JOE. Mullins?

ALEC. He that told on me.

JOHN JOE. How do you know?

ALEC. Our nice neighbours. And I never did anything on them.

JOHN JOE. Not at all, Alec.

ALEC. Well, I'd give Mullins a good belt in the head of a stick, but he'd have me up in court. Them are his ways.

JOHN JOE. Not at all. It was probably just a routine check-up.

ALEC. Routine check-up.

JOHN JOE. None of the neighbours would –

ALEC. Routine me granny. The neighbours are all right if you're down, but if you have anything at all, you can't die soon enough to suit them.

MULLINS *enters, making for his place in the shadows. He sees them.*

MULLINS. How ye! You'll be right in the morning, John Joe, to come to the bog with me? Looking well, Alec.

ALEC. Isn't it time for me, and I nearly seventy. The *pension* age.

MULLINS. Great man for your age all right. You had a visitor today, I heard? Hah?

ALEC. I had.

MULLINS. You had. Hah? Hah?

ALEC. I had. He was an educated man.

MULLINS. Yes? – Hah?

ALEC. He didn't have the ignorant ways.

MULLINS. Hah? Hah?

ALEC. I explained the situation.

MULLINS. Hah?

ALEC. All my people, I told him, were decent, respectable people, even if my mother wore a shawl going to mass itself! None of them ever informed to the soldiers one time for twenty-three shillings and got the legs shot off Danny Kelly! And none of them in later times did the quare thing to the huncyback girl in Clonshee, before they had to marry the horse-faced one from Ballinasloe side! And none of them ever had any truckin' with diseased auld hens, with the pip or pox or whatever they had, doing the Dublin merchants with their 'Spring' chickens! And none of them was ever brought up in court for one of them talking about football to the fish man, while the other was stealing the herrings from the back of his van! And none of them . . .

MULLINS *has fled the stage.*

ALEC. Well, not wishing him any harm now, not wishing him any harm at all, but may the two legs drop off him, the whore!

JOHN JOE. Ary, that kind of thing is no good at all, Alec. (ALEC's *anger is gone; he is tired.*) Come on. Come on into the house.

They go into the kitchen. MOTHER *is clearing away the buckets and bath, banging them about unnecessarily.*

ALEC. You heard, Julia?

MOTHER (*shortly*). I heard.

ALEC. Routine check-up, he says.

MOTHER (*rounds on* ALEC; *fiercely*). Yes! (*She stares defiantly at him for a few seconds. Then she continues banging things about.*)

JOHN JOE. I wouldn't worry, Alec, too much about –

MOTHER (*rounds on* JOHN JOE). And what's this I hear about you giving Peteen a hand with turf?

JOHN JOE. I just said I'd –

MOTHER. I just said I'd! Aren't you the generous boy! And the-curse-of-God-thing I seen you do around your own house for I-don't-know-how-long!

JOHN JOE. I was following your advice!

MOTHER (*words sound twisted and dirty*). I'd look well, pulling and dragging myself for *Peteen,* for *any* of them! – *Anyone*! – *Any* of *them*! – *Anyone*!

JOHN JOE. I was following your priest's advice!

MOTHER. *They'll* get by! The *Peteens* and the *Smiths*! *They'll* get on all right without you. *They'll* get by! But *us*, *us*.

JOHN JOE. I don't know what you're –

MOTHER. They'll all continue to scoff and laugh at us.

JOHN JOE. What are you talking –

MOTHER. Us! the way we are! All them sleekers scoffing and chaffing –

JOHN JOE (*shouts*). Shut your mouth! Shut your mouth. Shut your mouth!

MOTHER (*taken aback*). What are you saying to me?

JOHN JOE. . . . I didn't mean . . . I'm trying to . . . I . . . Well, something else for a change. They helped you once. All the work Mrs Smith did here one time when you were sick. And when Daddy was sick Peter Mullins sowed the garden one time, didn't he? I don't know what you are talking about.

MOTHER *is now crying.*

ALEC. Oh, I'm not a bit upset about it, Julia.

MOTHER. And you were better to us than anyone, Alec.

MOTHER *exits.*

JOHN JOE (*to himself*). I don't know what ye are talking about. What's on her now?

ALEC. . . . What's on any of them? . . . 'Tisn't the first time they did me damage . . . Oh, sure, one time, they were making out I was one of the boys that goes after the boys . . . Not that I minded that. But the priest, Fr. Daly, he was only a nipper at the time, came back to see me about the rumour. I told him the truth. 'I'm not', I said, 'your reverence. But I have all the same thoughts and dreams and urges as any celibate in the country.' . . . But I was too late in learning to speak out my mind when it was needed. There was always too many wheels spinning round in my head; and when all I needed was two: one to say yes, and one to say no . . . And I was fond of a girl. I forget what happened, but I remember her name . . . And I wanted to see Dublin. Just for a visit. But who would milk the cows. And sure I was well into middle-age before I realized that my father was in the house at all. And he could have milked them . . . But between one thing and another, and them whores watching every hand's turn I made, I'm the way I am, in that lonely house on me own, these thirty years. Oh, but, sure, don't I be cracking jokes for them? And I not wanting to . . . I don't like them . . . If I was a young man again, I'd – Ach! What's that to do with me now?

The two of them continue staring in silence into the fire.

Scene Eight

Friday

A pool of unreal light on the bedroom. JOHN JOE, *wide-eyed, alarmed, confused, is dreaming.* FR. DALY, MR BROWN, MONA, PAKEY GARVEY, MRS *and* AGNES SMITH, MULLINS, ALEC, MIKO, MOTHER *and* FATHER *are in and out of his bedroom, in and out of his bed, his dream, singly, en masse: Anything goes – well, almost anything. The stage is peopled with grotesque whispering figures throughout the dream.*

MIKO (*giggling*). Well, tee-hee-hee.

FR. DALY (*chuckling*). Yes, aw yes.

MR BROWN. I'm the richest man in town but the humblest.

MULLINS. Hah? Hah? Hah?

MIKO. Well, tee-hee-hee.

FR. DALY. Yes, aw yes.

MR BROWN. But the humblest, sir.

MRS SMITH. Craytures, mmmmm, darlin's.

MONA. Will we?

   JOHN JOE *discovers* MONA *beside him in the bed; she is scantily dressed and* FR. DALY *and* MR BROWN *are approaching.*

JOHN JOE. Hide! (*She hides under the bed-clothes.*)

MIKO. Tee-hee-hee!

FR. DALY (*to* JOHN JOE). Well, you little tootler!

   FR. DALY *and* MR BROWN *sit one each side of the bed.*

   Did you bring the scalpel, Malachy?

MR BROWN *produces a knife and a fork.*

Good man. And the lancet?

MR BROWN (*to* FR. DALY). I have it, Brendan.

FR. DALY (*to* JOHN JOE). Congratulations!

JOHN JOE (*gasps*). Ah?!

FR. DALY *with* MR BROWN, *turn to address the others.*

FR. DALY. Congratulations for being the great christian and holy-moreoever people that we are! Ever since 432 –

MR BROWN. A.D. he's talking about –

FR. DALY. Ever since that golden year –

MR BROWN. When St. Patrick came to Ireland –

FR. DALY. Look at all the things that's happened. Look at all the people called Paddy today!

MR BROWN. And I remember the time –

FR. DALY. A.D. you're talking about?

MR BROWN. People were going out and buying their cigarettes by the two –

FR. DALY. Yes, aw yes –

Mr. BROWN. Now they're buying them by the packets of ten! And by the packets of –

FR. DALY (*stops him with a wave of his hand*). Did you think of the cotton wool, Malachy?

MR BROWN. Aw Jaysus, I forgot it, Brendan!

FR. DALY *and* MR BROWN *hurry off. Now, incongruously,* MONA *appears from some part of the room – the last time we saw her she was concealing herself under the bed-clothes.*

MONA. Oh, please, please, please, John Joe, please, please, please!

MULLINS. Hah? Hah? Hah?

MONA. I love you, how I love you!

MIKO. Well, tee-hee-hee!

MONA. Oh God, how I love you! So will we, will we, will we, will we, please!

JOHN JOE. What, Mona?

MONA. Abscond!

MIKO. Bejingoes!

JOHN JOE. Hide!

> FR. DALY *and* MR BROWN *enter and exit briefly, talking urgently:*

MR BROWN. And by the packets of twenty!

FR. DALY. Yes, aw yes!

MR BROWN. By the packets of twenty, sir! (*They exit.*)

MONA. You're so virile strong, compatible wise, salubrious spring and adjacent.

Confusion of other sounds.

JOHN JOE. Just a second – Just a second! (*To collect his thoughts.*) One, two, three, four; one, two, three – Ah!

> *There is someone in the bed and it is not* MONA *and* MRS SMITH *is approaching.*

MRS SMITH. Craytures!

MONA. Will you marry me?

> MONA *appears to address this last remark to* PAKEY, *and* PAKEY *is making for* MONA *with evil intentions.* JOHN JOE *wants to intervene but* AGNES *now appears from under the bed-clothes, scantily dressed, to climb on top of* JOHN JOE.

AGNES. John Joe!

JOHN JOE. Aa, don't hurt me, Agnes, darlin'.

> JOHN JOE *and* AGNES *fall out of the bed and roll across the floor, locked in an embrace. They collide with* MONA *and* PAKEY *who are also locked together on the floor. And* MR BROWN *and*

FR. DALY *are now entering from different directions, each carrying a piece of cotton wool. And the other characters are making their own sounds.* JOHN JOE *breaks from* AGNES *and shouts:*

JOHN JOE. Stop!

Silence. Then, to gain further control, to himself:

One-two-three-four, one-two-three-four.

A moment's respite during which he tells himself.

It's only a dream, John Joe . . . (*To* MONA.) Isn't it?

MONA (*points at* MR BROWN). There's daddy: ask him for my hand.

JOHN JOE. Is he your father?

MONA. He is. Didn't you know.

JOHN JOE. I did. He's an awful nice man, so he is.

MONA. Ask him.

JOHN JOE. Will you give us Mona's hand?

MR BROWN. People don't know how well off they are, sir.

FR. DALY. Yes, aw yes!

MIKO. Well, tee-hee-hee!

MULLINS. Hah-hah-hah? (*etc.*)

JOHN JOE. Sir, I should be honoured if you would allow me holiest of wedlocks to your daughter Mona, in anticipation reply your earliest convenience, sincerely and truly, John Joseph Moran, youngest son of Tom Moran, grave-digger!

MR BROWN. Can you feed her in the way she's accustomed to feeding?

JOHN JOE. £98 a week, certainly.

MR BROWN. Have you money in the bank, are you well thought of? Are you a mass-server, choir-boy, in the Legion of Mary? Are you a teetotaller, non-smoker, non-consumptive and free of the palsy? Who are your people, I say who are your people? Any blue blood, red blood, sheeps' blood, black blood? Any insanity in the family? – have you a Communist in the cupboard? – have you a car? What are your chances of promotion? Do the neighbours see you going late to mass on Sundays? Any priests in your kin? – May-nooth men or foreign mission types? Any doctors, lawyers, teachers, vagabonds, blackguards, idiots, jailbirds, fiddlers? I say, any jailbirds? Have you been to uni, oony, bo-bo-bing, or West Point? How many letters have you after your name? Have you a gas cigarette lighter? Did you shoot Patrick Pearse? Do you know what a la carte means? Is your mother a washer-woman? Is your father a Greek scholar. Are you a genius? And who will make a suitable speech on your side of the family at the wedding breakfast?

JOHN JOE (*shouts*). A-a-a-a-a-a!

MR BROWN (*as he merges into background*). At the wedding breakfast, sir.

JOHN JOE. I'm not John Joe Moran!

MONA. O-o-o, John Joe!

MIKO. Tee-hee-hee!

FR. DALY (*coming forward*). Yes, aw yes!

MR BROWN. Dreamer, dreamer!

MONA. O-o-o-o, John Joe!

JOHN JOE. It's only a dream, Mona!

MULLINS. Hah-hah-hah?

FR. DALY. Get a ferret for yourself, John Joe.

JOHN JOE. M-o-ona!

FR. DALY. Listen to me, come here, what are you frightened about? Them are only the superficialities. Aw yes. Listen, the real issue, I'll tell you. There was a man in this town once called St. Patrick, and what's this he said to me now? Oh yes. 'You can go to hell', he said it straight out. 'Or you can go to heaven. One or the other, stay or go, it's entirely up to you.' Wasn't it a good one? But woe, says he, to the fooleen that goes to Holyhead way-woe, and leaves himself behind. Let the blackguards go. But let him not go that should stay; and let him not stay that should go. For, merrily, I would say unto that man: verily, watch me, look, and behold! – (*With sweeping triumphant gesture he sweeps the hold-all from under the bed and holds it aloft.*) I have a bag here for his soul. Woe! Cause he'll have to leave it behind him. We insist on that. Hand it in. I have a few nice ones in it already. Aw yes. The soul is not a thing to be bandied about in any old way or in any old place. Manchester for instance. Oh, before I forget to tell you, did you see the fooleen, Pakey Garvey the other day? Back from England, looking for his soul back. 'You can't have it', I told him. 'Why didn't you hand it in voluntary at the start', I said to him 'and it might be a different case! You know the rules', I said. 'So, there's no use asking for the impossible. Come back in forty years', I said, 'and we'll see if something can be done for you.' Off with him, his tail between his legs. Well now, you know what brought me back. (*He unzips the bag,* JOHN JOE *is starting to groan.*) You'll do the voluntary thing, John Joe, and you'll reap the benefits of that policy, and you'll feel lighter for it.

FR. DALY, *assisted by* MR BROWN, *with scalpel, lancet and cotton wool start to operate for* JOHN JOE's *soul.* MONA *comes forward to see what is happening.* JOHN JOE *has had his hands under his shirt. He now holds them in front of him, cupped, as if holding a bird. He is groaning; his eyes are closed.*

FR. DALY (*to* MONA). Turn your back, you. Don't be so curious. You're alright, Malachy. (*To* MONA, *approaching her.*) Didn't I tell you to turn the other way. All right. Off – off – off with you.

FR. DALY *and* MR BROWN *are ushering* MONA *off. The unreal light is changing to 'night' light.* JOHN JOE *is shouting.*

JOHN JOE. O-o-o! O-o-o! O-o-o!

MOTHER *enters, switching on the light. She is pulling on an old coat over her night-dress. She is barefooted.*

JOHN JOE. O-o-o! O-o-o!

MOTHER. What's on yeh?

JOHN JOE. I never did anything on them!

MOTHER. Dreaming. You're only dreaming.

JOHN JOE. I never did –

MOTHER. It's only a dream, a mac.

JOHN JOE. I want to do what's best!

MOTHER. A dream, a nightmare, John Joe.

JOHN JOE. I want . . . I want . . . I . . .

MOTHER. Sure, it's only a dream.

FATHER *enters in his underwear – vest and long-johns.*

FATHER. Wha'? What's on him?

MOTHER. Go back, you, to bed. He's all right. Go on. (*To* JOHN JOE.) You're all right now. Dreaming you were. I'll get you a cup of water.

MOTHER *goes to kitchen.* FATHER *follows.*

FATHER. Wha'? Dreaming is it?

MOTHER (*shortly*). Yes! Go back, you, to bed.

FATHER *stays in the kitchen.* MOTHER *takes a cup of water to* JOHN JOE. *He sips it.*

MOTHER. Are you awake right now? I thought when I heard the roars you might have a pain. That's your nerves. You aren't sleeping right anyway. Stay in bed tomorrow. And you shouldn't be reading them auld books I see around. Your eyes is sunk back in your head. Would you like a hot drink, John Joe? (*He shakes his head.*) Will I get you another cup of water? . . . Have you a headache? Will I get you pills?

JOHN JOE (*shakes his head*). What time is it?

MOTHER's *voice is soothing. She is not conscious of her emotional blackmail.*

MOTHER. It should be near striking four. I heard three ringing 'while ago, and two before that. Are you too hot? I took an extra blanket off our bed yesterday thinking you might be cold. There's white frost in places these nights. (*She tidies the bed and sits on it.*

Proudly.) I bumped into Fr. Daly again after his call here the other day, and he praised you up to the moon. He told me he had the highest respect for you, and for your word. He's all-in-all with Mr Manton, and you can be sure he'll get you in there, and you'll be secure in it if you mind it . . . He asked about your brother Frank too, and, sure, I had to say we had a letter from him last week with ten dollars in it. . . . I don't know, it was a bad day for poor Frank the day he went away. He knows the difference now . . . Eight dollars he sent home here ever. And that not even three pounds. I'm sure he'd like to come home. (*Tears in her eyes.*) If I had the money myself I'd send it to him. He'd send it to me if he had it. He was good once. But the company. And he didn't know what he wanted. Arguing, not content, and then fighting. He put a lot of wrong ideas into your head, too. He (FATHER) doesn't know he done jail, and you couldn't tell him . . . You can't tell him anything, but he'd be shouting and . . . Just shouting . . . Whatever is the matter . . . But you can be sure the neighbours knows all about Frank and they not seeing the postman coming near the house ever. And people living abroad sending the bad biteens out of the newspaper home to people living here . . . Sure, you're not thinking of going away? And everyone of Mr Manton's staff gets a fine hamper off him every Christmas.

JOHN JOE. Have you no slippers?

MOTHER. Ary what do I want of slippers? It's only the fooleens, going astray, that's running back and over to England. Everyone knows that.

JOHN JOE. We have to have something.

MOTHER. Yes. (*She looks at him.*) Everyone has to have something . . . You'll be all right. Keep in with your uncle. He's old now, and upset about the pension man. And he'll have to give up one or the other, the shop or the pension. (JOHN JOE *shakes his head.*) – But he thinks he will. He's frightened. (JOHN JOE *looks up at her big tear-stained face.*) It was me told on him. I did it for you . . . Try to fall asleep now. I've a few bob in the kitchen I was putting aside for the rates and I'll give you something out of it tomorrow evening. I'll scrape it up some way when the times comes. Are you all right now? And say a few prayers and go on to sleep.

She switches off the light and exits to her room. FATHER *comes from kitchen and stands outside* JOHN JOE's *door for a few moments.*

FATHER. Are you all right, John Joe, a mac?

There is no reply and FATHER *exits. Off, church bells ring four.* JOHN JOE *starts to cry softly.*

Scene Nine

Saturday

The hay shed. It is nearing dawn. JOHN JOE *and* MONA *are sitting on the hay. Pause.*

MONA. I was glad you showed up tonight . . . You didn't tell me where you were for the past few nights. It seemed like . . . ages . . . Do you know? You *are* a very bad court . . . John Joe.

JOHN JOE. Yes.

MONA. Did you think any more about going away?

JOHN JOE. No.

MONA. Are you feeling sorry for yourself or something?

JOHN JOE. What?

Pause.

MONA. Oh, do you know what Jimmy said to me once? Out in front of Daddy and all. We were sitting down to Sunday lunch and Jimmy was only eleven then. But he said, 'Mona', he said, 'I notice you have very good childbearing hips'. I was mortified. I was only a second-year at school and it was during the holidays, and –

JOHN JOE. School for young ladies with fat bullocks. Bullocks, I said, mind. Their daddiadies' bullocks at a hundred pounds apiece. What about me and Agnes Smith with thin chickens out in the back yard?

Pause.

MONA. Oh, and my best pal at school – (*She stops short; thinks.*

Then, almost a new Mona.) I want to talk to you. But how can I, with this – atmosphere – between us? And I have to say something, anything, the first silly old thing that comes into my head, to break it. It's childish. And I'm certainly not a child. I know what I want. And I have no – illusions. You must make up your mind. I know it's not because you're afraid. If it was that I wouldn't be here.

JOHN JOE. Oh? Thanks. That's great.

MONA. We can't keep talking about –

JOHN JOE. No, we can't keep talking about!

MONA. Well, that's all you're doing. I've made my decision.

JOHN JOE. And all I do is talk?

MONA. Yes.

JOHN JOE. Oh?

MONA. Well, do you think it's any easier for me?

JOHN JOE. That dress, can you enjoy it?

MONA. What?

JOHN JOE. I can't enjoy this sportscoat.

MONA. I know, I understand –

JOHN JOE. No. Do you feel guilty for every sip of a drink you take?

MONA. I know what you mean, but –

JOHN JOE. No, it's not that. Do you take a deep breath every time you get outside your own door? – Out of your own street?

MONA. Well, don't start feeling sorry for them.

JOHN JOE. Seeing corny pictures of them, martyrs. See? Do you feel that?

MONA. Are you boasting or complaining?

JOHN JOE. What?

MONA. There's a train out of here on Monday morning.

JOHN JOE. You don't understand.

MONA. I've money.

JOHN JOE. No! Lookity! (*Takes coins out of his pocket.*) I've money! Three whole full shillings and a sprazzy! (*Wanting to hurt her.*) Do you wish you could be poor for me? (*Turns away; to himself.*) It's not the money. (*Turns back to her; cynically.*) Aa, you're very nice, Mona. Mona, you're very nice.

MONA. What's wrong with being nice?

JOHN JOE. Aa, you're very – That Mullins! Them Smiths! Them – I'll kick the daylights out of them!

MONA (*beginning to cry*). We could hitch.

JOHN JOE. You don't understand at all. Do you feel guilty for every cigarette you smoke? And how can I do anything until I find out what's wrong with that?

MONA. We could leave.

JOHN JOE. It's not just a case of staying or going. It's something to do with Frank, and Pakey, and others like me who left. And others like Miko and Mullins and me who stayed. It's something to do with that. Does that mean anything to you? What exactly do you think of that?

MONA (*crying*). I think you're wonderful.

JOHN JOE (*stopped for a moment by her sincerity*). Oh – but – he – has – high – notions – you know, the gravedigger's son has! Ah yes: maybe that's all that's wrong with him. What are you crying for?

MONA. I'm not crying.

JOHN JOE. Fine – All right – Yes – Okay. (*He tosses away a coin.*)

MONA. You want to get rid of me, don't you?

JOHN JOE. What?

MONA. That would solve half your problem, wouldn't it?

JOHN JOE. Aw God! (*Then with a wild movement he throws away the remaining coins.*) Yes – It would – Right – Fine! I'm tired of it. This romance. We'll finish it! It's ridiculous. And let's hope they'll all be happy now. Come on. We'd better go. . . . Well, come on. It's dawn outside.

MONA. I hope you don't ever do this to any girl again.

JOHN JOE. Aw, for Christ's sake!

MONA. Well, I wouldn't give in.

JOHN JOE. You don't know anything about it!

MONA. I'm willing to take a stand –

JOHN JOE. What do I mean to you? No more than to anybody else. What do I mean to anybody else besides my mother, and what good is that? I've gone through this – 'love' – with dozens, hundreds of other girls. I've never felt anything for you. And I don't feel guilty or anything. You were the one who approached me one night. You mean nothing to me. You are a silly, stupid bitch. Whore if you could be. What means anything to you? Mummy, big farm, daddy; the priest plays golf with daddy; the bishop knows daddy; money in the bank. Where does John-Balls-Joe come in? For favours, pity? In a few years' time you'll give a nice little 'haw-haw' at all this. In love, Jesus, love! Come on if you're coming.

MONA (composed). . . . I'll go first. You'd better not be seen walking me home. (As she exits.) They might let me alone too now.

Scene Ten

Saturday – 3.00 p.m.

ALEC *sits outside the shop window staring dully at the ground. There is a suitcase at Moran's front door.* MOTHER *and* AGNES *are in* JOHN JOE's *bedroom.* AGNES *wears a new two-piece costume.* JOHN JOE *wakes up. He is not sure whether he is dreaming or not.*

MOTHER. Isn't this a nice how-do-yeh-do, Agnes? In bed at three o'clock on a Saturday afternoon. But, sure, coming in after the dawn. (*Explaining to* AGNES.) No. Dancing above in Athlone last night, and Tommy Ryan's car that a crowd of them were in broke down on the way home.

JOHN JOE *is smiling, waiting for an explanation for their presence.*

MOTHER (*laughs*). He doesn't know whether he's dreaming or not, Agnes.

JOHN JOE. Ah?

MOTHER. Agnes is off today. Didn't she keep it a great secret? (*He does not understand.*) Your poor mother, Agnes.

AGNES. I'm going to Dublin, John Joe, to get things settled up; and then I'm going out to America. Boston. I came to say goodbye.

MOTHER. I told her mother that you'd get up and take her case up to Fergusons'. Your mother's heart will be broken, Agnes.

AGNES. Will that be all right, John Joe? (JOHN JOE *nods.*)

MOTHER. 'Twill kill her.

AGNES (*to* JOHN JOE). I'm getting a lift to Dublin in Fergusons' fruit van at quarter past four.

MOTHER. 'Twill be the death of her.

AGNES. I'm twenty-eight years of age, Mrs Moran. (*Shakes hands with* JOHN JOE.) Goodbye, John Joe.

AGNES *goes out of the room and waits at the front door.* MOTHER *and* JOHN JOE *look at each other for a moment.*

MOTHER. Get up then, and deliver that case for her. (*She joins* AGNES.)

AGNES. Well, goodbye, Mrs Moran.

MOTHER (*embraces her*). Goodbye now, Agnes. Agnes, Agnes! Look after yourself.

AGNES *exits.* MOTHER *goes to rear of house for* JOHN JOE's *bicycle.* JOHN JOE *has remained in bed for a few moments, wondering is there irony in the situation. He jumps out of bed and dresses hurriedly.* MOTHER *brings his bicycle to the front of the house.* JOHN JOE *comes out of the house and gets on the bicycle. He is about to cycle off.*

MOTHER. The case! The case! (JOHN JOE *puts the suitcase on the bicycle.*) Come home straightaway now and I'll have a nice dinner ready for you. (*He cycles off.*) You ate nothing today!

MOTHER *looks after him for a few moments. Then she turns her attention on* ALEC. *She is moving towards the lifeless figure of* ALEC.

Scene Eleven

Sunday

About 1.00 a.m. JOHN JOE *and* MIKO *enter, walking with their bicycles, returning from the town. They are drunk. They stop as they approach Moran's house.*

JOHN JOE. No-no-no-no-no-no-no-no . . .

MIKO. What can be the matter with the man, I said?

JOHN JOE. No-no-no-no . . .

MIKO. Has he any consideration?

JOHN JOE. No, Miko; you let me down –

MIKO. Does he want, bejabers, to get me sacked for nothing? Tee-hee-hee. Has he any, what they call, espirit? And me with my neck stuck out a mile for la guillotine.

JOHN JOE. You let me down, Miko.

MIKO. I let you down? Well, bejingoes! Well, bejaney-mack-tonight! Well, you're a nice one anyway! Did you come to collect it at the appointed time and place? And I snook it out of the store on Wednesday morning. And haven't I compromised myself forevermore with Mary in Gavins' pub asking her to conceal it till you collected it? What will she be looking for off me in return? Won't I have to give her my all? Tee-hee-hee. And it was lying there in Gavins' all day Wednesday, and all day Thursday and all day yesterday. Be-the-hokies, when I called in for a quick one this morning and learned it was still there! What if it was uncovered by someone? What if my boss was in having a quiet creme de menthe with Michael T. Gavin, chatting about South East Asia? And Michael T., with an understandable hatred of cock-roaches, sees one scuttling under the bottom shelf. He bends with his mallet poised and, 'Hello! What's that nice little portmanteau doing there, Mary?' 'A portmanteau?' says my boss, interjecting, having an understandable interest in suitcases. What? Sure, I could have been arrested, in chains! Bejaney-mack-tonight, I said to myself, get it out of here lively, you'll get no satisfaction from John Joe Moran! And I snook it back to its own little nest in the store.

JOHN JOE. No, you let me down, Miko.

MIKO. What?

JOHN JOE. I'd be half way to London now if I had that case.

MIKO. What's coming over you? You were the bright lad. Are you going the way of all feather-heads?

JOHN JOE. I took you at your word, Miko.

MIKO (*suddenly angry*). And I took you at yours. Because I always thought you were earnest and knew what you were about and would do something. That's what I thought. And would a little fart of a suitcase stop you if you ever intended to make this gesture? No, I said, and I'm the fool to believe in anyone. Did he ever intend to leave? No, I said, he must want to stay here. And that's the long and the short of it, John Joe.

The speech has sobered-up JOHN JOE. MIKO *giggles nervously.*

MIKO. Up on your bike, Josephine! (*He goes on his bicycle.*) I'd better push off, as the fellow said, and sitting well in order, smite the sounding furrows! My mother will be out with a lantern. 'What does the clock say, Miko, son?' The cow says moo-moo, Mother, the duck says quack-quack, and the clock says tickety-tock! I'll see you tomorrow. (*Cycling off.*) 'For my purpose holds to sail beyond the sunset!'

MIKO exits. After a few moments JOHN JOE *goes into his house. MOTHER is waiting in the kitchen; bare feet; old coat over night-dress.*

MOTHER. You're not so early coming in.

JOHN JOE (*trips over a board entering the kitchen*). What's that doing there?

MOTHER. That's a new board to put a sign over the shop for you. It's yours now.

JOHN JOE. What?

MOTHER. I asked Alec, asked him out straight, since you and him in there (*FATHER*) is asleep. And you don't deserve it. (JOHN JOE *moves towards his room.*) Fr. Daly was here. (JOHN JOE *stops.*) He said to tell you to call down to see him when you came in. I'm sure he'd like to see you now at one o'clock in the morning.

JOHN JOE. What does he want to see me for?

MOTHER. And you got stranded outside Athlone last night, did you? And the car you were in broke down, did it, and you couldn't get home? Having the priest calling to the house in full view of the whole town twice in a week. The man you expect to get you a job!

JOHN JOE (*quietly*). Maybe I don't want him to get me a job.

MOTHER. Standing at the door talking to me for twenty minutes, and Peteen Mullins –

JOHN JOE (*quietly*). Peter.

MOTHER. Standing in the shadows, watching and listening. Peteen having his laugh.

JOHN JOE. Peter is his name.

MOTHER. Staying out all night with that streeleen above in the bank. (JOHN JOE *goes to his room.* MOTHER *follows.*) Oh yes! Oh yes! That oinseach –

JOHN JOE. Girl!

MOTHER. That oinseach! And I seeing her myself tonight, walking out the Dublin Road with the young schoolteacher. (JOHN JOE *is surprised.*) Yes, yis, yis! Linking him! Out the Dublin Road! Oh, sure, doesn't she love you. Didn't I see the letters from her in your pockets, addressed to Mr Brown's shop. Doesn't she love you?

JOHN JOE. Yes.

MOTHER. Doesn't she *love* you?

JOHN JOE. What's wrong with that word?

MOTHER (*mimicking*). What's wrong with that word. Wait on, till Fr. Daly sees you.

JOHN JOE. What – does – he – want – to – see – me – for?

MOTHER. What does he want to see me for? You're rotten! That's what you are! Oh yes, that's a nice way for anyone to be carrying on. Rotten!

JOHN JOE. What's a nice way for anyone to be –

MOTHER. Joe-een Ryan, with another lebidjeh, had his name bally-ragged to the country when he had to marry his filthy street-walker on a Saturday night.

JOHN JOE. That's what I was at last night?

MOTHER. Are you going to tell me you were dancing above in Athlone.

JOHN JOE. I'm not going to tell you anyting. You and Fr. Daly and the neighbours have it all worked out.

MOTHER. I'm finished with you anymore. Slaving away here for you. Eating only half-enough myself, while –

JOHN JOE (*shouts*). I don't want anyone slaving for me!

MOTHER. Keep your voice down.

JOHN JOE. I never asked it! Jesus, I'll be thirty-four years of age next month, and you keep talking as if I was a child!

MOTHER. Well I know what you are!

JOHN JOE. What do you want of me?

MOTHER. . . . I don't want anything off you! Keep your voice down and don't be getting him up.

JOHN JOE. Daddy! Daddy!

MOTHER. Talk quiet.

JOHN JOE. Daddy! Daddy!

MOTHER. Your father then, your father. Don't be getting your great father up!

JOHN JOE. Well, why isn't he here talking to me?

MOTHER. Do you want to wake up the whole street?

JOHN JOE. Why is it you?

MOTHER. Oh, shout then, shout! Give the neighbours more to scoff
and rhyme about. The Morans! Lord! The Moran-eens! The
Moran-eens!

JOHN JOE. Yes! 'Cut the snail's head Moran!' 'Dig a cold bed;
Morans are going to bury the dead!' Is that bothering you?
Childish talk, ignorant talk, no worse than your own!

MOTHER. What are you saying to me?

JOHN JOE. The house is filled with your bitterness and venom. A
person can hardly breathe in that street. I don't know what started
it. Whether it's just badness or whether it came from a hundred
years ago, or whether it's your ideas of sex, or whether it's –
(MOTHER *is crying.*) No, you'll listen to me –

MOTHER. What are you saying to me, John Joe?

JOHN JOE. No! You'll listen to me for a change. No good crying
or making faces or –

MOTHER. The neighbours, Lord –

JOHN JOE. You'll listen to –

MOTHER. Getting them up to their windows and –

JOHN JOE. All right then. I'll put your mind at rest about what
the neighbours know and hear, once and for all. Then maybe we
can talk.

MOTHER. John Joe!

JOHN JOE (*goes out front door to the road*). Can you all hear better
now? Because I wouldn't want you to miss this valuable news.

MOTHER (*crying at the door*). Will you come in and don't be
disgracing us.

JOHN JOE. Mrs Smith! Jack Smith! Are you in position? Peter!
Mrs Mullins! Alec! I have valuable news for you. Pay heed!
Listen. You saw the priest here this evening. No, it wasn't about
the job he's trying to get me. I spent all night in Fogarty's hay
shed last night with a girl called 'streeleen' that's working above
in the bank. I raped her. Out all night with her, what else could

it be? 'Twas lovely. Tell everyone. We have flour-bags sewn together for sheets. My mother asked Alec for the shop today. She has one pound three put aside for the rates. Oh, but we know Mrs Smith doesn't use a sheet at all. Did you know that Mrs Smith? We know that from the day Peter Mullins climbed in your back-room window, because it was the only room in your house he hadn't seen. But he said it was clean, but he wouldn't give you two-pence for the sticks of furniture. And what else? Oh, the rig-out Mrs Mullins had on last Wednesday wasn't new at all; a cast-off, bought by her sister in Seattle off one of them cheap-jacks they have over there, for thirty-eight cents. And that she doesn't sleep with Peter; and hasn't for a number of years. Oh, come on, come on, shout out what other valuable newses you want.

FATHER *has got up and is arguing with* MOTHER *inside the door.*

JOHN JOE. There must be other things. Frank! My brother Frank done jail in America. Fourteen months, drunk and fighting a policeman. Say a prayer for him. Oh yes. That Mrs Smith let Agnes go with only a five pound note and her ticket. And we know Mrs Smith has £582 in the post-office. And in her *own* name.

FATHER (*calls*). John Joe!

JOHN JOE. And a few things I know for myself. That shopboys in the town are not interested in two-shilling bribes, or any bribes, from decent people for writing down on their bills one shirt or one pair of shoes instead of two. And another thing: That Peter Mullins's job is not so secure. That the insurance inspector has had complaints about broken confidences. That everybody knows about the amount of everyone else's policy. And I know that the Egans back the road, who started with nothing, and who are now getting on well with their furniture business closed their accounts in the shops in town tonight. That they will be shopping in future in Galway, fourteen miles away. Do you think it's because they're stuck up? And what else? Let me think of the other valuables I have to say.

FATHER, *now with an overcoat over his underwear, is at the door with* MOTHER.

MOTHER. Sacred Heart, will you get him in!

FATHER. Didn't you start him off?

MOTHER. Get him in! – Get him in! And don't you be doing the amadan on it too.

FATHER. John Joe!

MOTHER. Get him in!

FATHER *approaches* JOHN JOE.

JOHN JOE. And that Mrs Quinn is buying sweets for her children by the box. By the box! Isn't she grand? In spite of all the free chocolate her children were getting passing up and down this road, in exchange for information.

FATHER. John Joe.

JOHN JOE. And what else of value have I?

FATHER. Come on in now.

JOHN JOE. The cartwheel. Do you want your cartwheel back?

FATHER. Wha'?

JOHN JOE. Jack Smith! My father wants that cart –

FATHER. No! No, a mac!

JOHN JOE. Are you sure?

FATHER. I am.

JOHN JOE *goes into the kitchen, followed by* MOTHER *and* FATHER.

MOTHER. Mother of God! Lord! We're disgraced!

JOHN JOE. We are a disgrace.

MOTHER. Drink! Drink! Auld slobs of porter, worse than the tinkers!

JOHN JOE. No, I'm sober.

MOTHER. With that other drunken sleeker, Miko Feely.

JOHN JOE. Miko put me right tonight.

MOTHER (*making for her room*). Well, are you satisfied now?

JOHN JOE. No. Can you wait a minute, Mammy?

MOTHER. Are you satisfied now?

JOHN JOE. Can we talk now?

MOTHER. The spectacle you made of us before the world. We're well showed up now! The way we are! Now they know! And about your brother! Poor Frank! Lord! . . .

JOHN JOE (*waits to see if she has finished*). Yes. Poor Frank, and the way we are. We are badly off. And there are people trying to do something about it, and not getting much help. And some other people like it this way because we are a proof of their fortune. And there's some of ourselves like the pigs, happy and glorying in it, maggots – feeding on this corpse of a street. Wives and husbands up and down the road, pots calling kettles black; the poor eating the poor. Anybody's business but our own. Not content with the hardships of today, the poor-mouth whining about yesterday as well. Begrudging, backbiting, hyprocrisy; smothering and slobbering in some cunning 19th century way. And you thought you'd keep Frank here like that?

MOTHER. Well, you'd better follow your brother if that's the way you feel.

JOHN JOE. You – drove – him – away! And Pakey Garvey didn't want to go. And it wasn't the money. It isn't a case of staying or going. Forced to stay or forced to go. Never the freedom to decide and make the choice for ourselves. And then we're half-men here, or half-men away, and how can we hope ever to do anything.

FATHER. Well, if you've finished talking you can make your free choice now.

MOTHER. We're not forcing you to stay.

JOHN JOE. No. Nor I'm not being forced to go either.

JOHN JOE *goes to his room.*

MOTHER. Another sleepless night for me. I'm not going to get a wink.

FATHER. You'd better stay there then.

FATHER *exits*. MOTHER *follows after a few moments.*

Scene Twelve

Monday morning

ALEC, *lifeless, seated outside the shop window.* MOTHER *and* MRS SMITH *are getting water at the pump.*

MRS SMITH. Aaaaa, a graw, I'll miss her! Godeen help us Mothers!

MOTHER. But isn't it a lovely Spring morning!

MOTHER *goes into house.* MRS SMITH *sniffs at the Spring air, looking up at the sky and the birds. Then, as she exits:*

MRS SMITH (*miserably*). Birdeens: craytures! Mmmmm!

JOHN JOE *comes out of house carrying the new signboard. He goes to* ALEC.

JOHN JOE. Well, Alec!

ALEC (*do not look up*). Get whatever papers there is to be signed and I'll sign them.

JOHN JOE (*mock haughtiness*). Oh, I don't think so. If you are willing to pay me, I might consider giving you a hand in my spare time. Maybe open a grocery and tobacco department. People around here are walking a quarter of a mile for their groceries.

MULLINS *enters.*

MULLINS. Good morning, Alec. Good morning, John Joe.

JOHN JOE. Good morning, Peter.

MULLINS *exits.*

JOHN JOE. And knock that wall in there and let the counter run the length of the house. And that ridiculous window! But maybe you're too old. Anyway, a little pokey hole of a shop like yours is no good to me. It might have been good enough for you, but it's certainly not good enough for me. (ALEC's *head is up in anger.*)

I'm going up town to get a job for myself.

ALEC. Well, go! (*He is on his feet.*)

JOHN JOE. I will.

ALEC. Well go!

JOHN JOE (*laughs*). I will! And I'm going to open a bank-account too with a girl I know.

JOHN JOE *exits.*

ALEC. And take your auld board with you!

He has taken up the sign-board to throw it after JOHN JOE. *Then he sees the face side of it, on which is printed 'ALEC F. BRADY'. He looks after* JOHN JOE *and chuckles:*

ALEC. Oh, the whore!

He turns his attention to the shop window, guaging it critically. He is trying out the new sign-board as the lights fade.

On the Outside

Written with Noel O'Donoghue

On the Outside received its first professional stage production at the
Project Arts Centre, South King Street, Dublin, 30th September, 1974,
with the following cast:

KATHLEEN	Biddy White Lennon
ANNE	Bairbre Dowling
JOE	Donal Neligan
FRANK	Chris O'Neill
DRUNK	Brendan Cauldwell
MICKEY FORD	David Byrne
FIRST MAN	Willy Collins
GIRL	Angela Harding
BOUNCER	Gerard O'Brien
SECOND MAN	Mick Quinlivan

Director Tom Murphy
Designer Gerry O'Donovan
Stage Manager Flo Daniels

The time is 1958, and the place is outside a country dancehall.

A quiet country road outside a dancehall. The dancehall, in the background, is an austere building suggesting, at first glance, a place of compulsory confinement more than one of entertainment. Then, through a small window, high up on the wall, can be seen the glow of the ballroom lights, and, occasionally, to complement the more romantic numbers, a revolving crystal ball, tantalizing and tempting to anyone on the outside without the wherewithal to gain admission. Popular music of the time (late fifties) played badly by the band, continues throughout the play, except from time to time when a dance ends. Then follows some half-hearted applause, and this in turn is followed by the faint buzz of voices. The usual dancehall noises.

A placard is placed somewhere against the dancehall wall, and its message reads: 'I.N.T.O. DANCE TONIGHT, 8-12. MUSIC BY THE MARVELTONES ORCHESTRA. ADMISSION 6/-.'

There are two girls on the stage when the lights come up: Kathleen and Anne. Anne is the younger, about twenty, very naive and anxious to be conventional. She is sincere but rather stupid; the words of a popular song are the true expression of the human spirit. Kathleen, on the other hand, is two years older and more sophisticated. She has, perhaps, worked in Dublin or England for a time. She has less romantic illusions, is more neutral and even cynical at times. But that is not to say that she is unromantic. She simply has a better idea than Anne of what it is all in aid of.

When we first see them, Anne is rather dejected, looking off towards the main road half-hopefully. Kathleen is walking up and down. She has a cardigan pulled tightly over her shoulders. They have obviously been waiting for a long time. Kathleen stops and looks at Anne.

KATHLEEN. It's late. (*Pause.*) Well, don't you think you've waited long enough? We're here I-don't-know-how-long.

ANNE. Just another few minutes.

KATHLEEN (*to herself*). Just another few . . . It's late!

ANNE. He'll be here any second now. I'm sure of it.

KATHLEEN. Yes, when the dance is over, I suppose. And that won't be very long at all now. Lord, I'm frozen.

ANNE. It's not that cold.

KATHLEEN. And I left off that heavy vest too. I hope my mother doesn't find it under the pillow. And will you look at the cut of my shoes! Oh, come on in. It's silly waiting any longer.

ANNE. Ah, Kathleen, a few seconds more.

KATHLEEN. He's not coming.

ANNE. But why? He said he would. It was he wanted to. He said to meet him here outside the hall.

KATHLEEN (*impatiently*). Yes – yes, but he's kind of late, isn't he? (*There is a short pause; KATHLEEN sees she is having no effect.*) What's his name anyway, Frank what?

ANNE. . . . But he's very nice though.

KATHLEEN. Are you sure his first name is Frank even? . . . What does he do? What kind of job has he?

ANNE. Ah, Kathleen.

KATHLEEN. Oh, you never can tell. I was going with a fella last year in Dublin. Not bad looking either. And, of course, fool here was real struck. I liked him. Richard Egan. And then one night we met – ych know Mary O'Brien nursing in the Mater? And later she took me aside. 'Do you not know who he is?' she said. 'No.' 'He's the porter at the hospital.' The shagging porter. *And* his name wasn't Richard.

ANNE. What was it?

KATHLEEN. Declan . . . I don't remember what he told me he was. The Civil Service I suppose. Taught me a lot I can tell you . . . What did this Frank tell you he was?

ANNE. He said he was – he didn't say.

KATHLEEN. What?

ANNE. He isn't like that. He really is very nice.

KATHLEEN. Tck!

ANNE. We – talked to each other.

KATHLEEN. Talk! They're all the same. (*Moving to a better vantage point.*) . . . Wait on: someone coming now.

ANNE. Is it him?

KATHLEEN. I can't make him out so well. It might be.

ANNE. Oh, what'll I say? What'll I do?

KATHLEEN. Up near the car park.

ANNE. Come on in, Kathleen – We're going in – We're not waiting a second longer – Come on.

KATHLEEN (*still looking off right*). Oh, it's not him at all. He's gone up the other way.

ANNE (*disappointed*). Are you sure?

KATHLEEN. Some old drunk. They're everywhere. Well, we might as well go in so.

ANNE. Ah, Kathleen.

KATHLEEN. What's wrong with you now? You were mad to go in a few seconds ago.

ANNE. I can't understand it.

KATHLEEN. He's forgotten, he's with someone else, he's drinking. In some pub.

ANNE. I don't like men who drink.

KATHLEEN. The dance is half-over –

ANNE. I asked him and he smokes alright –

KATHLEEN. He isn't coming –

ANNE. But he doesn't drink, he said.

KATHLEEN. You're only a fool.

ANNE. . . . But why?

KATHLEEN. For god's sake, don't take him so seriously: You've only seen him once before . . . Look, I'm sure he's very nice, but he'll hardly come tonight now. There's thousands of them in there! Maybe you'll meet someone with a car.

ANNE (*childishly*). I don't want a car . . . I don't agree . . . I don't care what he does.

KATHLEEN (*giving up*). I don't know, I'm a worse fool to be waiting here with you at all.

ANNE. Do you think . . . could he . . . have come, maybe, and didn't see us here and gone in, thinking, maybe, I wasn't coming?

KATHLEEN (*to herself*). In the name of –! (*Seeing her chance.*) Yes. That's what happened. We'll go in and see. Come on. Well, come on.

ANNE (*reluctantly*). Alright.

KATHLEEN (*as they exit*). Good job you brought your own money with you.

The stage is empty. There is a short pause. Then JOE *comes in. He looks at the hall entrance.*

For the record, JOE *is about twenty-two and employed as an apprentice to some trade, as indeed is* FRANK. *He is immature and irresponsible but not bad.*

JOE (*calling softly off*). Alright, sham, they're gone.

FRANK *enters. He is a stronger personality than* JOE. *Same age as* JOE *and works at the same trade. He is old enough, however, to be aware of the very rigid class distinctions that pervade a small, urban-rural community and resents 'them' with the cars and money because he has not got the same. It is hard to say how far he is really bad and how far he is only an intelligent product of his environment.*

JOE. Blazes, I thought they'd never go. I've cramps all over from being stuck back there.

FRANK. What did you think of her? Not bad, is she?

JOE. Not too bad for this hole, I suppose.

FRANK. Ah, she's alright now.

JOE. Wait'll you see the one I'll get. (*Starts to move towards door.*)

FRANK. Stall, sham, take it easy a while. We don't want to land in right after them.

JOE. Hey, what are you going to say to her? . . . You kept her waiting all night . . . Tell her you're an automatic scientist and you were ducking communists all night. If she's a bit innocent, she'll swallow anything.

FRANK. Stall it, stall it.

JOE. Tell her the truth so. I was hiding behind the wall all night watching you because I hadn't got the price of two tickets. That'll go down well.

FRANK. Pity I didn't work the see-you-inside act, but she thinks I'm loaded. The car we came in broke down and we only got here now.

JOE. And she'll say: 'Who did you come with'? And you'll say – oh, Mickey Ford or someone. And she'll say: 'Oh, de Mickey de Ford or someone: we saw de Mickey de Ford going in at nine o'clock.' What's all the fuss about this one for anyway, she's only a mul.

FRANK. I just want something she'll believe. I wouldn't mind hanging on to her for a while. What would you tell her?

JOE. Slap her down.

FRANK. I'll tell her what I like and she'll believe me. And I'll be narked she didn't wait for me.

FRANK *breaks into song.* JOE *dances, then stops when he sees the poster.*

JOE. Hey!

FRANK. What?

JOE. How much is this dance tonight, did you say?

FRANK. Four bob.

JOE (*points at poster*). The poster. Admission is six bob.

FRANK. Six *what!*

JOE. Six shillings. You and your four bob dance. Where did you get that from?

FRANK. It's robbery. (*Laughing.*) Six bob!

JOE. Just because there's no other dance on around here tonight.

FRANK. Well, we'll just have to pay up since we came this far. Give us two bob till Friday.

JOE (*laughs*). What? And how do you think I'm fixed?

FRANK. You'll get it back Friday.

JOE. Give you hell. I've four and six. Four and a lousy kick. And I borrowed that just before I came out here.

FRANK. Are you coddin' me?

JOE. Where would I get it?

FRANK. Great, that's great, that's just deadly now. I've just the bare four bob. (*Pause.*) The quare one in the box-office?

JOE. Will I give her a twirl? (*'try-her'*). Give us your money.

FRANK. Offer her half-a-dollar apiece first: we might get in for four then.

JOE (*adjusting his tie*). We might get in for choicer (*nothing*) yet.

FRANK. Okay, Elvis, go to it.

> JOE *moves up the steps into the hall.* FRANK *takes out his cigarettes immediately* JOE *has disappeared, and lights one. Noises are heard off stage and the* DRUNK *enters. He is a small, labouring man, aged about fifty. He shuffles on stage, sees* FRANK *and approaches him.* FRANK *treats him in a very off-hand manner.*

DRUNK. Excuse me. Excuse me – Sir! (FRANK *ignores him.*) Excuse me. Give us a light, will you? (*He has a cigarette in his hand.* FRANK *still ignores him.*) Could you oblige a gentleman with a light, Sir? (FRANK *gives him a light.*) Thanks. Much obliged. Thank you. (*Notices music in background.*) What's on?

FRANK. Dance.

DRUNK. Hah? A dance? Oh, a dance! . . . Who's playing it? Who's playing the music?

FRANK. Marveltones.

DRUNK. Marbletones – Mar – Marvel (*Laughs.*) I thought you said the Marvel – Marble – tones. (*He laughs.*) How much is it?

FRANK. Six bob.

DRUNK. Hah?

FRANK. Six bob. Six shillings.

DRUNK (*still unaware of* FRANK's *annoyance*). Hah?

FRANK. One, two, three, four, five, six shillings.

DRUNK (*looking at him seriously for a second in silence*). No need to be smart, young fellah. No need at all. You can answer a civil question when it's put to you.

FRANK. Go away.

DRUNK. No need for that. No need.

FRANK (*controlling himself*). Right, no need. Now will you clear before I call the guards or something. Go home to your wife. Go home.

DRUNK. Home? Anything but the death! (*He grins.*)

FRANK (*looks at him for a moment, then walks away*). . . . Look, don't be annoying me.

DRUNK. And I've no wife. I'm single. No one in the world but me. No one cares. I don't care! . . . Why did you say –

FRANK. Okay, okay, you've no wife. Now will you go.

DRUNK. Where?

FRANK. Anywhere.

JOE *comes out of the hall.*

FRANK. Any good.

JOE. No good, no luck, no cut: six bob.

FRANK. Bitch.

JOE. If the hall was empty they'd be damn glad to take it.

FRANK. Bloody crowd of robbers.

DRUNK. What's up lads?

JOE. We might try her again later on though.

DRUNK. What's up lads?

JOE. Who's the sham?

DRUNK. How ya goin' on, young fellah?

FRANK. Oh, my pardon. Ten thousand, one hundred and eighteen pardons! This gentlemen here is Mr Narrow-Neck.

JOE. How yeh, Mr Narrow-Neck!

DRUNK. Hah? No – no, I said – I said –

FRANK. You didn't? Sorry about that, sham. I thought the name suited him, didn't you? (*They laugh.*)

DRUNK. No, I said –

JOE. Little-Back, he said. Delighted!

DRUNK. No, I said –

FRANK. No, you didn't. Are you drunk or something?

JOE. You'd better watch out, Mr Little-Back, or you'll be seeing gollies next: Waw – waw – aw!

DRUNK. I said Jim Daly. Jim Daly. Seamus O'Dálaigh.

FRANK *and* JOE *laugh.*

FRANK. Ah, of course. I knew I'd seen you before. Muscles himself: Mr Universe of 1958. Well, Mr Daly, meet my friend here (*Points to* JOE.) Bill Bottle and goodbye now. Scram, do you understand? Scram! Scram!

JOE *takes* DRUNK's *cap and throws it deftly at dancehall door.* DRUNK *follows his cap and exits to hall.* JOE *laughs then becomes silent.*

JOE. Well he's in and we're here.

FRANK. Was she anyway promising at all? (*Nodding towards box-office.*) Boxy.

JOE. We'll try her again in a while.

FRANK. Who do they think they are with their little post-office books and two and a half per cent, per annum.

JOE. Anno Domini, Annie get your gun.

FRANK. This one ass place.

JOE. And she got her gun. (*Then suddenly.*) We're the asses to come out here miles. Six bob! And the floor like corrugated iron in there.

FRANK. Lord, I'd love to be independent. . . . I have to get in.

JOE. You won't see me paying six bob.

FRANK. What do you think?

JOE. Could we get pass-outs maybe?

FRANK. Yeh . . . (*To himself.*) Yeh, cadge and cadge again.

JOE. There's a good crowd in there. There's bound to be someone leaving soon: jiggy-jiggy in the passion wagons.

While JOE *is saying the last line above,* MICKEY FORD *comes out of the dancehall. He is about the same age as* FRANK *and* JOE. *His suit is better than theirs and he wears a loud American-style tie. He is well off, having a car and no lack of money. He is a tradesman of some kind or at any rate he has a good job. Nevertheless, he is adolescent in many ways. He likes to talk about himself and boast of his exploits in a rather naive way. This smugness and boasting make him very self-confident and lead to an appalling triviality in his conversation. Naturally, neither* FRANK *nor* JOE *can bear him since he represents all that they are not and all that they resent. He affects a slight American accent whenever he thinks of it.* FRANK *and* JOE *watch him go up the road.*

FRANK. Oh, look out: there's Handsome himself! Whid (*look at*) the tie he has on.

JOE. How yeh, Mick!

MICKEY. Hi, fellahs! Are you going in?

FRANK. ⎫ Yeh.
JOE.   ⎭

MICKEY (*exiting to a shop off*). See you inside. (*They laugh quietly at his disappearing back.*)

JOE. Think would he – would he be any good for the touch?

FRANK. No.

JOE. Well, we can't wait for someone to come along and say, 'here, lads, here's three-and-six for ye'.

FRANK. And he'll tell half the hall inside we touched him. His money, you know, is real special. He's loaded to the nockers with threepenny bits – legacy stakes.

JOE. Well, I'm going to try him when he comes back. If he tells anyone we touched him we won't give him the money back: Law three hundred and six in the touchers' rule book.

FRANK. Do you see him driving round the town always with one arm sticking out the window? Hail, rain or snow the elbow is out. I don't know how he doesn't get paralyzed with the cold. I'm going to write to Henry Ford.

JOE. Yeh?

FRANK. And tell him to invent a car – great idea – with an artificial arm fixed on and sticking out the window. The hard man car they'll call it. Then fellahs like Mickey can still be dog tough without exposing themselves. Get me?

They laugh.

JOE. Stall it. Brilliantino is coming back.

FRANK. Are you happy at your work?

JOE *whistles furiously in reply.* MICKEY FORD *enters, eating an apple.*

JOE. Oh, there y'are, Mick!

FRANK *nods.*

MICKEY. Hi fellahs! (*He comes over to them.*)

JOE. What's the dance like, Mick?

MICKEY. Not bad. The band's not bad.

JOE. Much women inside?

MICKEY. Loaded, stacked, powerful talent, deadly. Best I've seen for a long while.

FRANK (*dryly*). I bet you've squared already, Mick?

MICKEY. I've my eye on a few but I don't know which I'll bother with yet. There's a Jane in there that's nursing in England home on holidays. What a woman! Full of your arms, you know. (*He winks.*)

JOE. There's nothing like the ones that spend a while in England. Them are the ones to get.

FRANK. And the Protestants.

MICKEY. And she's all talk too. Ah, but I don't think I'll bother.

FRANK (*innocently*). Jay, and I bet you'd be sound there too, sham.

MICKEY. Sure I know. But there's a few others I'm sort of watching.

FRANK. Yeh?

MICKEY. There's a Kelly one in there from round here. I had –

JOE. Anne Kelly?

MICKEY. Do you know her, Joe?

JOE (*looks at* FRANK). Sort of.

MICKEY. I had a dance or two with her. I was thinking about her but – I don't know.

JOE. Why?

MICKEY. Ah – there's not an awful lot of her in it. Do you know her, Frank?

FRANK (*nods*). How's the car going, Mick?

MICKEY. A bird.

JOE. Any accidents or anything?

MICKEY. No, but do you know, I was coming home from work the other evening. Monday. Well you know me – boot down all the time.

FRANK (*dryly*). You were doing over fifty, I suppose?

MICKEY. Fifty? Sixty-five, seventy. I was flying along. All of a sudden I felt the pull to the right. Like a flash, I changed down and slapped on the brakes. The front tyre was gone.

FRANK (*whistles*). Wheeew!

MICKEY. They're tubeless, you know.

FRANK. Go on!

JOE. Jay!

MICKEY. Well, you know yourselves when you're speeding like that and you get a blow-out, the car could go anywhere. Heaven, hell, anywhere. You just want to stay cool and act fast. It's easy enough to get killed nowadays.

JOE. That's if you're not fast enough like you were?

MICKEY. Gee, guys, you want to be fast alright.

FRANK. That's for a blow?

MICKEY. For any emergency, and for a blow-out too. Which reminds me, I'd better blow. (*All laugh.*) I've a real nice bit asked for the next dance.

JOE. Good man, Mick – Oh Mick, a second! You see we're kind of stuck, like, and –

MICKEY. Aw jay, lads, the car is full!

JOE. No. We're okay for getting home: we're stuck for a few shillings.

MICKEY. Aw jay, lads –

JOE. Three and six –

MICKEY. Aw jay, lads –

JOE. Till Friday night – Friday dinner time.

MICKEY. I couldn't. I've – I've only five bob on me and I've to get a gallon of juice for the bus going home. And it might be a roundabout way too. (*He smiles slyly but gets no response.*)

JOE. Maybe you'd manage without the petrol?

MICKEY. I couldn't, honest. She's very low. I had five and sevenpence and I bought the apple. The good stuff costs five bob a gallon.

JOE. If you give us three and six we'll borrow it inside for you. There's a crowd from home in there.

MICKEY. Aw, I couldn't risk it.

JOE. We'd be sure to get it! There's no risk.

MICKEY. Aw, it's too chancey. Look, I'd like to help you but I can't. I've a few odd pence here if that's any use to –

FRANK. Okay.

MICKEY. Jay, sorry now, fellahs.

JOE is about to try again.

FRANK. Okay!

JOE. Okay, sham.

MICKEY. Sorry. I'd better go in. Be seeing you.

He goes into the hall.

JOE. You have your glue. Twilix. (*He joins* FRANK). Where did he get that accent. 'Hi, fellahs'.

FRANK. He has an uncle in America and they get letters at home from him. . . . He'll be all double bases and carburettors and ignition keys inside now with the women.

JOE. And they seem to fall for that kind of bull too. He squares a lot – (*pulls a lot of women.*)

FRANK. I don't know does he square that many. A lot of the women he gets are very thick anyway. The car helps . . . He mustn't give anything up at home at all.

JOE. By God, it's not so with me. That auld fellow would break my back.

FRANK. How much do you give up?

JOE. Half . . . How much do you give up? (FRANK *sighs.*) . . . But they need it.

FRANK (*pause*). And what do you do with the other half? A pound!

JOE. Spend it! (*They laugh.*)

FRANK. Aw but – Jesus! – this bumming around from one end of the week to the other is terrible! Jesus, look at us now! Look at

us in that auld job with Dan Higgins. The fags we get out of him
– just from soft-soaping an imbecile. Ah, yes, we all get a big
laugh but – I don't know.

JOE. Did you see Dan Higgins today going into the boss's office?
(*Laughs.*) He nearly tore the head of himself pulling off his cap.

FRANK. But again it's not so funny. No, serious, sham. This old
job. Do you know what I think? Do you know what the job is like?
Serious, sham.

JOE (*laughing*). What?

FRANK. The bosses are gods and we're only –

JOE (*laughing*). Carney, the transport boss –

FRANK. No, but the job. You know, it's like a big tank. The whole
town is like a tank. At home is like a tank. A huge tank with walls
running up, straight up. And we're at the bottom, splashing
around all week in their Friday night vomit, clawing at the sides
all around. And the bosses – and the big-shots – are up around
the top, looking in, looking down. You know the look? Spitting.
On top of us. And for fear we might climb out someway – Do you
know what they're doing? – They smear grease around the walls.

They laugh. Pause.

FRANK. It's pushing on. We'd better do something quick.

JOE. Will I try Mary Jane in the office again?

FRANK. I don't think so.

JOE. What?

FRANK. . . . Joe.

JOE. Yeh?

FRANK. It's no good standing out here. If one of us went in he
could borrow money for the other.

JOE. Or if he had a date inside he could go off with her.

FRANK. Look, sham, give us two bob and I'll get it for you inside.
This Anne Kelly – look, sham, if I don't get in there I'm finished
with her.

JOE. So what?

FRANK. I'll get the money for you inside.

JOE. Who'll give it to you?

FRANK. I'll get it.

JOE. Do you think I'm going to be standing around out here, frozen, on my tod?

FRANK. I'll only be a second.

JOE. No.

FRANK. It's the only chance we have. Listen, I have to go in there: You heard Ford yourself: He has his eye on her.

JOE. Alright so. I'll go in and borrow the money for you. Give me one and six.

FRANK. No, I've a better chance.

JOE. I don't see that.

He exits for a few moments to investigate the possibility of getting in by means of a back way. Noises and voices arguing are heard from the box-office. JOE *returns.*

JOE. Hey, what's up?

FRANK. It must be a ladies choice: the women are charging Ford!

JOE. It's a bull and cow! (*A row.*)

They move to a better vantage point as dancehall door opens and BOUNCER *appears pushing* DRUNK *out of the hall.*

BOUNCER. Out! Out!

DRUNK. Come out, come out! Come on out, you and all the other bastards in there!

BOUNCER. You watch your language around here now, Daly.

He exits returning to dancehall.

DRUNK. I want my bottle back! No one takes anything from me and gets away with it! I'll show yeh! (*To himself.*) Mr Tough. God, I'd kill him. Steal their lousy booze. (*He sees* FRANK *and* JOE.) Did you see that? I'm telling you he's lucky I didn't – Did you see that?

FRANK. I thought you'd tear him to pieces.

DRUNK. I would too. (*Shouts.*) And I will!

JOE. What were you going on with the girl for anyway?

DRUNK. Hah? What girl? There was no girls.

JOE. At your age, too, McGoo.

DRUNK. No, no, the booze was –

FRANK. What were you doing to her?

DRUNK. It was the booze.

JOE. Come off it!

DRUNK. No! I had a bottle of stout in my pocket and I was just having a quiet slug when up comes Tough. Mr Big Tough comes up and says I stole it. I didn't. 'Twasn't me.

JOE. Stole what? Your bottle?

DRUNK. Naw! The band's booze. Someone stole it, all of it – the whole case of it! But 'twasn't me. They blamed me. They put me out and said it was me.

FRANK. That band is failing alright.

DRUNK (*puzzled*). Hah?

FRANK. Right, we'll see you to-morrow.

They ignore DRUNK. DRUNK *begins to move away. He tugs up his trousers and money rattles.* FRANK *and* JOE *look at each other.*

FRANK. Oh, Jim?

DRUNK. Hah?

FRANK. That chucker-out wants his ears pinned back alright.

DRUNK. And I told him. I told him I never set eyes on it.

FRANK. Sure –

DRUNK. I'm not one for drinking that much – a case of it!

JOE. Sure.

FRANK. Jim, old stock, you know the three of us should stick together. Pals.

DRUNK. Pals.

FRANK. Joe, that chucker-out can't get away with insulting people like that. I'll tell you, we'll go in and get stuck in him.

JOE. Cripes, we will. Come on. Oh, how much is the dance?

DRUNK. I don't know. I paid –

FRANK. It's six bob.

JOE. I've only four and six.

FRANK. Wait a minute. (*Produces his money.*) Four lousy bob.

JOE. We're only short three and six. Just three and six.

FRANK. That's all that's stopping us from Chucker-head. A lousy three and six.

DRUNK. Short of cash, lads?

JOE. Three and six.

DRUNK (*mournfully*). Lousy three and six.

FRANK. A friend is what we need now.

DRUNK. Well, I'm your pal, amn't I?

JOE. Sure!

DRUNK. Well, I'm your pal, amn't I?

FRANK. The best, Jim. You won't see us stuck.

DRUNK. I wo'ont. How much do ye want?

JOE. Three and six.

DRUNK. Three and six. (*He takes some coins from his pocket and hands them to* JOE.) Here.

FRANK (*to* JOE). How much is in it?

JOE. Hang on.

DRUNK. Here's more. Take it. (*Handing more coins.*)

FRANK. How much is in it?

JOE (*to* DRUNK). Is that all you have? (*To* FRANK.) Sixpence halfpenny.

FRANK. What?

DRUNK (*still searching*). That's all. All gone now, pals. Have ye enough? Then don't worry. We'll get him. We'll wait here till Mr Tough comes out after the dance to get him.

FRANK. Go home.

DRUNK. Hah?

JOE. Get home!

DRUNK (*as he exits*). Home. Scram. Pals. Well, I'm not going home. . . .

JOE (*turns to look after* DRUNK). Jays, like a stray dog! . . . What brought us out here? What clown told you it was a four bob dance?

FRANK. Stall – Wait – two coming out now.

A couple, man and a girl, anywhere between twenty and thirty years of age, come out from dance and start to move off. They have been given passes by the BOUNCER *in case they want to go back again.*

GIRL. I thought we were going to the shop?

MAN. I just want to get something in the car for a minute.

JOE. Hey, any pass-outs?

MAN. No. Not a soul fainted. (*He grins proudly. The girl laughs.*)

FRANK. ⎫ Haw-haw! Funny man! Big joke! Pity about your face!
JOE.   ⎬ Makum joke for squaw! Waw! Buff! The wit! Half wit!

FRANK. Great old fun wasn't he?

JOE. God bless him.

FRANK begins to whistle idly. JOE *rattles the money in his pocket and idly takes out a box of matches, looks at them and quickly replaces them. He moves up and down giving an occasional kick to the ground.*

JOE. Oh, to have a lickle house, to own the hearth and stool and

all, in the dear little, sweet little emerald Isle, in the county of
Mayo.

Pause.

Break down the bridge six warriors rushed,
and the storm was shot and they shat in the storm!

FRANK. And Sarsfield strung up by the nockers behind them!
(*Pause.*) Look, let me go in and borrow the money for you.

JOE. Now don't start that again.

FRANK. It's the only sensible thing to do.

JOE. Will I try the quare one in the office again.

FRANK. I'll try her.

> FRANK *exits into hall.* JOE *takes out cigarettes and lights one
> quickly. He takes several deep pulls furiously in order to make the
> cigarette smaller. The couple (that exited on p.194) re-enter, the girl in
> a minor huff adjusting her clothing. At the same time,* BOUNCER
> *appears in dancehall doorway, ejecting* FRANK.

BOUNCER. Out! Out!

FRANK. No need to break my effing arm!

BOUNCER. What's that?

FRANK (*walking away*). Okay, Jim.

BOUNCER. You watch your filthy tongue and keep away from here
if you know what's good for you.

> *Couple and* BOUNCER *exit to hall.*

JOE. What happened?

FRANK. Boxy in the office got ratty and called the bouncer. Jim.
(*Roughly.*) Give us a fag.

JOE. It's only a butt, I had, sham.

> FRANK *gropes in his pockets and produces a butt. A second couple
> come out of the hall. The girl is* KATHLEEN. JOE *runs over to them.*

JOE. Are you going back again?

SECOND MAN (*curtly*). No.

JOE. Any chance of your pass-outs? – We'll buy them.

KATHLEEN. That your friend over there?

JOE. Yeh.

KATHLEEN. Is he Frank?

JOE (*doubtfully*). Yes.

KATHLEEN. I was with a girl tonight who was waiting for him.

JOE. Is that – ah – so? (*He does not know how to handle the situation.*)
Frank! Come here, a minute, sham. This here is a friend of Anne
Kelly's.

FRANK. Oh, hello. Oh yes.

THIRD MAN. What's up?

KATHLEEN. Just a minute. (*To* FRANK.) She was very disappointed when you didn't come.

FRANK. Yes? Is that so? You see, we were held up. I was
disappointed too. Is she inside?

KATHLEEN. She waited an awful long time for you.

FRANK. Yeh? Well. She shouldn't have waited so long.

JOE. In the cold too.

FRANK. I hope she wasn't mad at me.

KATHLEEN. I don't know. Maybe *she'll* understand. You're going
in aren't you?

Slight pause.

JOE. Well, if you give us the –

FRANK (*cutting in quickly*). We were playing a football match. Oh,
only a sort of a street league, you know. But they take that kind
of thing so seriously, you see? And the match started late too. I
was vexed but what could I do – you know? – togged out there –
I just couldn't – you know?

JOE. And it was nearly eight o'clock when –

FRANK (*cutting in again*). Yeh. And then to crown it all – you know how before a match you've no right place to put your clothes – and I gave my money to one of the crowd to hold for me and – well, the match finishing so late I just fired on my clothes and dashed out here and forgot all about the money. I knew Anne would be waiting and I didn't want to keep her that long, so –

KATHLEEN. Then you haven't any –

FRANK. Oh, any other time, you know – you couldn't forget to collect a thing like that – but it was so late and it never entered my head and I didn't want to keep Anne so long.

KATHLEEN. So you haven't any money?

JOE. That's why we want pass-outs.

SECOND MAN. Well, you can have ours. (*He gives them to* JOE.)

JOE. Thanks.

FRANK. Thanks very much. I hate to –

SECOND MAN. That's alright. So long. (*He's trying to get away.*)

KATHLEEN. Oh, you'd better hurry.

FRANK. Yes?

KATHLEEN. Competition.

FRANK. Me? Who?

KATHLEEN. Bye.

SECOND MAN. Bye.

KATHLEEN *and* SECOND MAN *exit.*

JOE. So long.

FRANK. So I've competition.

JOE. Wonder who it is.

FRANK. Ford. Well, we'll soon take care of that. Come on. Give me one of those passes. Act casual-like now, like as if you were in before.

They go into the hall. The stage is empty. Slight pause.

JOE'S VOICE. We were in before!

BOUNCER'S VOICE. Get out! You weren't in before!

FRANK'S VOICE. We were!

BOUNCER'S VOICE. Outside the two of you! Quick now! I've had enough of you all night.

BOUNCER, FRANK and JOE *appear at the door.*

FRANK (*holding up his pass-out*). And what are these things meant to be for?

BOUNCER. You watch your filthy tongue!

JOE. What are pass-outs for?

BOUNCER. Give them to me. (*Takes* JOE's.) They're not transferable.

FRANK (*pleads*). Aw, Jim. We'll slip you eight bob.

BOUNCER. You don't know me, don't use my name therefore. (*Pushes them away.*) Now clear.

JOE (*an undertone*). Now clear before Johnny MacBrown swallows his false tooth.

BOUNCER. What? . . . Did you pass a remark? . . . (*To* JOE.) Are you a good man? . . . (*To* FRANK.) Are you? . . . Maybe you're two good men, hah? . . . Townies . . . Clear. (*His challenge not accepted, he exits to hall.*)

JOE. . . . Will we blow?

FRANK. These buffers will soon object to us walking on the roads. He wouldn't be so tough in town.

JOE. I thought earlier the pass-outs wouldn't work.

FRANK. Yeh-yeh-yeh-yeh-yeh, you knew it all. (FRANK *regrets the remark, he takes out his last two cigarettes; he would like to smoke one and give the other to* JOE: *the futility of it. He puts cigarettes back in his pocket.*) God, these buffers! (MICKEY FORD *enters. They do not see him.*) Like as if we were dirt.

JOE. . . . Will we blow?

MICKEY. Hi, fellahs.

JOE.
FRANK. } Hi!

MICKEY. Gee, guys, hot in there. Girl inside talking about you, Frank. Anne Kelly.

FRANK. Yeh?

MICKEY. You had a – sort of a date with her.

FRANK. Sort of?

MICKEY. Are you thinking of going with her?

FRANK. What business is that of yours?

MICKEY. I mean – She knows you're out here.

FRANK. How does she know? Did you –

MICKEY. I didn't tell her. I –

FRANK. Mouth! Listen Ford, no one else would have told her.

MICKEY. I didn't – I just came out to –

FRANK. Ah, shut up. You'd better keep well away from me from now on because I'd love to hurt that handsome face.

MICKEY. God, I'd give you more than you'd want anytime. (FRANK *gives a short derisive laugh.*) But I have my brothers inside tonight –

FRANK. Your brothers – Your big brothers – The crankshaft family! You give me a pain in my royal differential arse!

MICKEY. They're inside. And you remember you have a long way to go home.

FRANK. And you remember they're only home on holidays, and in a week or two nice little Mickey-bags will go home some night with his Florida Beach tie all blood. (*He grabs at* MICKEY's *tie and gives it a tug.*)

MICKEY. God, you won't try anything like that on with me. Think back what happened with you and your auld drunken auld layabout auld fella last year: oh, didn't quiet, cunning Frank stand beside him kicking in the shop window, and stand beside him wanting to take on the town. The priest saved you from being arrested but he mightn't bother a second time.

FRANK. How many girls have you squared tonight, sham?

MICKEY. I've Anne Kelly squared. Do you think she'd have anythin' to do with you now?

FRANK *moves towards him.*

MICKEY. You'd better to stay where you are.

FRANK. Pity about his head – isn't it, Joe?

MICKEY. I'll be out in a –

FRANK. Tell us about the blow-out again, sham.

MICKEY. I'll be out in a minute with her. If you know what's good for you, you'll – well, you know what's best to do. Remember my brothers will be just inside the door. (*Exits quickly into hall.*)

FRANK. I'll get him. I'll get him.

JOE. Not tonight, Frank.

FRANK. I'll get him, I'll kick the day-lights out of him.

JOE. Take it easy –

FRANK. I'll make him sorry.

JOE. The brothers. Four of them.

FRANK. I'm not an eejit. They'll be back in England in a week or two.

JOE. What's so special about this Kelly one anyway.

FRANK. . . . Ah, she can go to hell. I'm not sticking around here much longer. England. I'm bailing out of that lousy job. Lousy few bob a week. Twenty-two years old and where does it get me? Yes, sir – I'm a pig, sir – if you say so, sir! (*Suddenly.*) Well, he's not getting away with her that easy.

JOE. But –

FRANK. Don't worry – don't worry.

JOE. But he'll call the brothers –

FRANK. No. By now, he'll have told her how hard a man he is – how he can break a fellah's back with a spit. I'll chat her up when she comes out. (*He stands watching the door.*)

JOE. Let's blow, sham.

DRUNK *enters.*

FRANK (*to* DRUNK *intensely*). You! Keep away from me!

JOE (*to* FRANK). You want to chat her up? Here she is.

MICKEY *and* ANNE *come out.*

FRANK. Anne. Anne! (ANNE *stops.*)

MICKEY (*nervously*). Leave her alone.

FRANK. I can explain. Honest to God, I was playing football. Honest to . . . No. I hadn't the money. Am I leaving you home?

MICKEY. What about all the lies you told her? Pick on someone your own class now.

FRANK. Ford, there's nothing surer but I'll get you.

MICKEY. Now, Miss Kelly – there's Frank Mooney. What do you think of him? (ANNE *is crying now.*)

FRANK. Am I taking you home? Anne?

ANNE. . . . . You're only a liar. I wouldn't have anything to do with you. (*As she exits.*) Are you coming, Mickey?

MICKEY *exits after her.*

FRANK (*quietly*). . . . Shout at them.

JOE. What?

FRANK. Shout, shout, shout at them!

JOE (*roars*). Spark-plug face! Handsome! Glue-bags!

FRANK. Torn mouth!

JOE. Carburettor head! Cop on yank!

FRANK. Torn mouth! – Torn mouth! – Torn mouth! (*Laughing harshly, drawing* DRUNK *into their company.*) Wait, he's in top gear now! – She's not tickin' over so good. Valve timing out, I'd say – condenser is faulty. Going round a corner, bootin' her to the last, doin' seventy three and a half miles an hour and do you know what happened him? – Do you know what happened to him? A cock of hay fell on top of him! (*They laugh harshly.*) Oh, this – this damn place, this damn hall, people, those lousy women! I could – I could –

He rushes over to the poster and hits it hard with his fist. He kicks it furiously.

JOE. Come on out of here to hell.

They exit. The band plays on. DRUNK *is giving a few impotent kicks to the poster as the lights fade.*

On the Inside

On the Inside was first produced at the Peacock Theatre, Dublin, on 18th November, 1974, with the following cast:

MISS D'ARCY	Colette Proctor
ANGELA	Deirdre Lawless
KIERAN	Donal Neligan
MALACHY	Brendan Cauldwell
MARGARET	Bairbre Dowling
WILLIE	John Olohan
SEAN	Gerard O'Brien
BRIDIE	Maureen Aherne
MR COLLINS	Geoffrey Golden
MRS COLLINS	Billie Morton
FIRST MAN	Tony Lyons
SECOND MAN	Patrick O'Callaghan

Dancers: Valerie Belton, Mary Dowling, Colm Daly, Larry Murphy.
Director Tom Murphy
Designer Gerry O'Donovan
Stage Manager Bill Hay

The time is 1958, and the place inside a country dancehall.

A dancehall. Only a part of the dancehall is visible to the audience. The scene favours one end of the hall where there is a soft drinks bar or a lemonade table. Doors to the ladies and gents cloakrooms on either side of the soft drinks bar. A poster on a wall reads: 'I.N.T.O. DANCE. MUSIC BY THE MARVELTONES. ADMISSION 6/-.'

A dance in progress. People on the periphery of the dance floor watching the dancers: ladies on one side, men on the other. Dance ends: usual clapping and dancehall noises. One of the girls standing by, wearing an overcoat, is MARGARET. She is about 20, a depressed, hangdog thing about her. MISS D'ARCY and ANGELA, two teachers, come out of the cloakroom. MISS D'ARCY is in her thirties, a little neurotic, staccato-voiced, given to prefacing her remarks with nervous little double-coughs. ANGELA is nineteen, ponytailed, pretty, and innocent in a breathless sort of way. The men standing by are WILLIE, a bankclerk, an eager-eyed, speedy, young ladykiller. FIRST MAN, about thirty. And SECOND MAN, in overcoat, his back to us all the time. (Perhaps SECOND MAN becomes SEAN later in the play.)

MISS D'ARCY. Do you see anyone you like?

ANGELA. Not yet.

MISS D'ARCY. They're only a bunch of mullackers . . . Aren't they?

ANGELA. Yes.

MISS D'ARCY. Pulling and dragging a person. And they're worse outside. A fellow last week had me up against a wall. I thought he was going to – I thought he'd – He nearly strangled me! No finesse. Your dress is lovely.

ANGELA. Yours is – nicer.

MISS D'ARCY. Made it myself.

ANGELA. . . . . Here's Mr Collins.

MR COLLINS (*to* MRS COLLINS). The kids were all asleep when I was coming out.

MISS D'ARCY. How yeh, Tom. Hello, Molly.

MRS COLLINS. Hello.

COLLINS, *about fifty, the headmaster, dressed in overcoat comes from dancefloor with his wife, MRS COLLINS, leading her to the soft drinks bar. She is about forty; wears a dress. COLLINS has a watchful, though impassive, face; given to chewing his false teeth behind closed lips; a rather taciturn cheerless man; a habit of not looking at people when he speaks to them. His wife is at her best when he is not with her.*

MR COLLINS. It's (*the dance is*) only mixed middling.

MRS COLLINS (*going behind mineral bar*). Excuse me.

MR COLLINS. Six bob was too much.

ANGELA. Isn't she great to do the mineral bar?

MR COLLINS (*nods*). Enjoying yourself, Angela?

ANGELA. Yes. Thanks.

BRIDIE *enters wearing overcoat and exits to ladies cloakroom. She is about twenty-five, a good lot of make-up, a good figure; home on holidays from England. Men's heads – WILLIE's and FIRST MAN's – turn to watch her. And WILLIE goes a step further, positioning himself more advantageously for her return.*

MR COLLINS. . . . Only mixed middling.

MISS D'ARCY. A right bunch of mullackers. Look at that little squirt there.

MR COLLINS. Who's he?

MISS D'ARCY. God's gift to women. He's working in the bank above in Caltra. 'Who are you, where do you come from, what do you do'. The same old thing. The cheek. No finesse.

MR COLLINS. Oh look in. The pubs must be closed.

MARGARET, *also, reacts to someone off, approaching, and she exits to ladies' cloakroom. KIERAN and MALACHY enter, circling the edge of the dancefloor, watching the girls. KIERAN is about twenty-three or twenty-four, a teacher; a charcoal-grey suit. MALACHY is in his thirties; an experienced layabout. MALACHY wears an overcoat. Both have drink taken. For the record, more than likely, MALACHY has never had sex.*

MR COLLINS (*a greeting*). The pubs must be closed!

MISS D'ARCY. How yeh, Kieran!

KIERAN. Peg. Angela.

ANGELA. Hello.

MR COLLINS. I bet you've spent all your backpay over the weekend?

KIERAN. No.

MALACHY (*joining them*). Beside yon straggling fence that skirts the way, with blossomed furze unprofitably gay, there in his noisy mansion skilled to rule, the village master beats his little school, he said!

He leaves them to take off his overcoat and put it under a chair.

MR COLLINS. That layabout is still as thick as ever. What are you knocking around with him for?

MISS D'ARCY. Where's the girlfriend?

KIERAN. Oh she's – she's coming. I think.

MR COLLINS. She's here. Or I think it was her I saw. Be in on time now in the morning and let it not be like other Monday mornings. Oh you should have seen him a few weeks back. Twenty minutes late Angela, his class roaring like bulls, and nothing but a foolish grin on his face. You must be getting your oats from that Ballinasloe lassie.

MISS D'ARCY. Oh, Tom! (*Laughing.*)

MALACHY (*joining them*). A man severe he was, and stern of view; I knew him well, as every truant knew. Mr Collins, Miss Darcy! Miss Quinn, I believe? Still beating the children up there?

MR COLLINS. We didn't succeed in beating much into you.

MALACHY. The *board* of education.

MR COLLINS. Will you dance Angela? (*To* KIERAN.) And listen, buy a car for yourself now and don't be borrowing mine, destroying it every Sunday night.

MISS D'ARCY. Oh, Tom!

MR COLLINS. What?

MISS D'ARCY. Destroying the back of the car.

MR COLLINS. D'yeh hear?

KIERAN. Will do.

MR COLLINS (*moving off to dancefloor with* ANGELA). Do you think you'll make a fist of the teaching? . . .

Pause. MISS D'ARCY *waiting to be asked to dance.* MARGARET *enters from ladies' cloakroom and moves across background, affecting to be unaware of* KIERAN's *presence.*

MALACHY. There she is, the girlfriend, Ciarán.

MISS D'ARCY. She mustn't have seen you.

MALACHY. Well, he's a terrible pig of a man.

MISS D'ARCY. Who?

MALACHY. Curley Wee.

MISS D'ARCY. Excuse me.

KIERAN. Sure, Peg.

MISS D'ARCY *goes to soft drinks bar.*

MALACHY. Sure. Jasus, I'd be afraid of that one! Does she do the trick?

KIERAN. Aw, Malachy.

MALACHY. Jasus, she'd have a cheek not to!

KIERAN. What did you think of Angela?

MALACHY. Three or four years too old for me. The girlfriend is throwing the eye this way.

KIERAN. She rang today, so I said, come along, yeh know, if she liked. Sort of.

MALACHY. God, you'd want to watch it there. The habit of time got many's the good man in the end.

KIERAN. Sure I know. Still, a fella wouldn't like to see another fella with her afterwards.

MALACHY. What?

WILLIE *asks* MARGARET *to dance. She refuses.*

KIERAN. This is a dreary old caper. No, she rang me today and said – Well I think it's a funny thing to say to your boyfriend – And she said, I wonder if we could meet. Hmm? We've been meeting every Sunday night for – Hmm?

MALACHY. Beware of the eyes of March, as the poet said. A pregnant class of a statement that.

KIERAN (*laughs*). God, what would a fella do then! (*But* MALACHY's *remark makes him think.*)

MALACHY. But, hey, you haven't spent all your money, have you? (KIERAN *displays a few pounds from his top pocket.*) Because we could do with a naggin or two later on. This early closing is uncivilized.

BRIDIE *enters from ladies' cloakroom.* WILLIE *is over to her like a shot, asks her to dance and leads her to the dancefloor.*

MALACHY. Bow-wow! Bow-wow! What's that? Look at the pair of josies on that! Look at little Willie wrapping himself around that! (KIERAN *makes some grimace of distaste.*) What?

KIERAN. It's ridiculous. Only disgracing himself.

MALACHY. What?

KIERAN. We're all only disgracing ourselves.

MALACHY. What are you talking about?

KIERAN. This Sunday-night job. (*He demonstrates the close dancing style.*) And if not that, we're lurking somewhere; in doorways, or dirty old sheds, or mucky old laneways.

MALACHY. You're a bit – what is the word? – down tonight. And you shouldn't be: the tankful we've had. I've been noticing it all evening.

KIERAN. Disgraceful. Well, it doesn't suit me.

MALACHY. A professional man.

KIERAN. If you like, yes. Not pulling rank now or anything, but I find it –

MALACHY. Dis-gusting.

KIERAN. Well, look at it this way –

MALACHY. Bow-wow, bow-wow, look at it again! (*BRIDIE*)

KIERAN. A few years ago: out in the open with it –

MALACHY. The great outdoors, the furry glen, or forninst the haystack!

KIERAN. No. But you'd get maybe half a dozen kisses of an evening and you're in love. But then, when the rest of it starts – Yeh know? –

MALACHY. The rummagin'.

KIERAN. Yeh. That's all we progress to. Fronts of cars, backs of cars, doorways, steering wheels, gear-levers, and love starts to fade, and we've had our chips.

MALACHY. The hammer job, is it, you want to do?

KIERAN (*sighs*). . . . I'd better go over. (*He does not move.*)

MALACHY. Is it the quare one beyond you're talking about?

KIERAN. No. No, I'm talking generally.

MALACHY. Metaphysically.

KIERAN. But how does a fella get out?

MALACHY. Honour.

KIERAN. What?

MALACHY. Honour. The best way I know. Honour, which is economics. Look, the fella says, I'm very sorry but there's a financial consideration to be made here, and, I'm not up to it. To which she replies, I suggested it before and I do so again: we pay every second turn. As a man, the fella says, my honour cannot allow that. Then a quick jump, for auld times' sake, and you're gone. A tragedy, yes, but the best of friends must part. Look, I'll go and have a search for the bootlegger, and see you back here. Jasus, will you look at that again! I'm going to wheel that tonight.

MALACHY *goes off in search of 'The Bootlegger'.* KIERAN *joins* MARGARET.

KIERAN. Hello.

MARGARET. Hello.

KIERAN. . . . Oh, I'm fagged.

MARGARET. What?

KIERAN. Fagged . . . It's a dreary old caper . . . That a new dress?

MARGARET. No.

KIERAN. Hmm?

MARGARET. I've this old thing since last year.

KIERAN. It's – It's very becoming . . . You're quiet tonight.

MARGARET. I was just going to say the same about you.

KIERAN. . . . Any news? (*She shakes her head.*) What? . . . A bit of Ballinasloe scandal maybe?

MARGARET. No.

KIERAN. You said you wanted to –

MARGARET. Oh. (*She sighs.*)

KIERAN. I was wondering if we could meet.

MARGARET. What?

KIERAN. That's what you said.

MARGARET. When?

KIERAN. On the phone. Yes. I was wondering if we could meet. Like, I think that's a funny thing to say.

They continue looking at each other – he hawkishly; she, trying to remember.

Hmm?

MARGARET. I wanted to see you.

KIERAN (*nervously*). Yeh?

MARGARET. . . . Lonely.

KIERAN. What?

MARGARET. I was lonely . . . I was thinking about when we started going out first.

KIERAN. Forty years ago.

MARGARET. No. It'll be seven months next Sunday.

KIERAN. Yeh?

MARGARET. Oh, I don't know. I feel you don't like coming to see me now.

KIERAN. Did I say that?

MARGARET. No.

KIERAN. I have to borrow a car –

MARGARET. A few months ago –

KIERAN. The headmaster's car – the price of petrol –

MARGARET. You said you'd always get to see me –

KIERAN. Thirty-two miles –

MARGARET. That there would always be a way . . . There's a big difference now, isn't there?

KIERAN. Is there?

MARGARET. We've come a long way.

KIERAN. Yeh?

MARGARET. I thought that things would change after – Recently.

KIERAN. After what – after what?

MARGARET. Nothing.

   Pause.

KIERAN. Of course we've come a long way. Of course things

change. All things change. Everything. But it doesn't mean anything. Things – change. That's all . . . Hmm? And that's the news now?

MARGARET. Could I have a cigarette?

KIERAN. Alright. You were just feeling depressed.

MARGARET. Thanks. (*For cigarette.*)

KIERAN. And that's the news now? – But you don't smoke! What?

MARGARET. I don't inhale them.

KIERAN. . . . What?

MARGARET. I was just thinking –

KIERAN. Thinking and then saying things and then phoning up the school the next day apologizing for spoiling the night, etcetera.

MARGARET. I don't know what's coming over me with my moods lately.

KIERAN. The trouble with you is it has to be fairytales all the time. (*He begins to relax, whistle with the band.*)

MALACHY, *accompanied by* SEAN – 'The Bootlegger' – *enter.* SEAN *is aged anything from twenty to thirty.* MALACHY *motioning to* KIERAN.

MARGARET. Love you.

KIERAN (*absently*). What?

MARGARET. Love you.

KIERAN. Look, will you excuse me for a minute, I'll be back in a second.

MARGARET. If you like.

KIERAN. No need to be that way about it. I just want to see someone over here. I'll be back in a –

MARGARET. If you like!

He stays with her. MALACHY *and* SEAN *join them.*

MALACHY. How are things in Ballinasloe?

MARGARET. Fine.

KIERAN. How yeh, Seán.

SEAN. How yeh, Kieran.

Pause. MARGARET *moves a few steps away.* FIRST MAN *asks her to dance. She dances with him.*

SEAN. I've only a few quarter bottles.

MALACHY. Either your employer J. J. Dillon and Son, is going to end up bankrupt in a month or you're going to get six months.

KIERAN. How much?

SEAN. Fifteen bob.

KIERAN. My eye!

MALACHY. Two quarters for a quid. No haggling. (*They agree.*) Can we afford it Ciarán?

KIERAN. Port? Port? Whiskey! (*The transaction is made.*)

SEAN. Did you hear about your man in Galway? A fella called Wilson: he used be always at the dances in Seapoint.

MALACHY (*indicating a low-sized man*). Jimmy Wilson?

SEAN. Yeh. Seven of them he's put in the club.

MALACHY. Seven!

SEAN. Seven! Up the pole! Over the holiday season, in three months.

MALACHY (*indicating Jimmy Wilson's size*). Jimmy Wilson?

SEAN. I'd swear my oath, Kieran, he isn't that size.

MALACHY. And the same man lying on his back, dying with T.B. last year! Who were the birds!

SEAN. There was a Daly one, a Lyons one, a Mannion –

MALACHY. Knew her.

SEAN. Burke.

MALACHY. Yep.

SEAN. A Quigley, and I didn't know any of the other two. And do you know where he was knocking them off?

MALACHY. Where?

SEAN. In the furnace room at the back of that church near Seapoint.

MALACHY. The lock on that place was broken for years. All you had to do was – (*He demonstrates.*) Now! And the priest in that place was the guy who used to be out letting the air out of the tyres of the cars parked around there at night. Poetic justice.

SEAN. But wasn't it shocking?

MALACHY. Dusty, Johnny, dusty.

KIERAN. What happened to him?

MALACHY. He scarpered?

SEAN. They ran him out.

MALACHY. Well, they could hardly make him marry them all!

SEAN. And he had a good job. But they ran him.

MALACHY. Jasus, a medal I'd have given him! But he'll be remembered.

SEAN. He'll be remembered. I'd best continue my rounds before I get down to business. Hey, did you see the big young one with the big jugs? –

MALACHY (*warning*). That game's preserved, sonny.

SEAN (*leaving them*). A pleasure to do business with you.

MALACHY (*to* KIERAN *who is taking a slug of neat whiskey*). Steady on Ciarán. Mrs Collins is on the whiddin' key: We don't want her to see you drinking neat malt. (*To* MRS COLLINS.) You haven't a drop of soda-water or anything dangerous like that there, have you?

MRS COLLINS. You're a right pair!

MALACHY. We'll settle for the aqua pura so, Molly, if himself isn't around.

MRS COLLINS. And all the lovely girls over there to be dancing with!

MALACHY. Quite so, Molly. But first, but first, with the aid of this potatation – Would you like a drop? – we're endeavouring to ascertain the essence of love, so that we understand what we're about. Your health, Molly. What would you say love is?

MRS COLLINS. Oh, sure, love is a lovely thing.

MALACHY. It's a very – what is the word? – beautiful thing.

KIERAN. At the start.

MRS COLLINS. Are you alright, Kieran?

KIERAN. But then it gets –

MALACHY. In-con-venient.

KIERAN. Yeh.

MRS COLLINS. Why don't you just have a glass of water, Kieran?

KIERAN. But where does it go?

MALACHY. What?

KIERAN. A few years ago – One time – A long time ago I'm talking about now – Not to have to sleep for a whole year: just to keep looking at her.

MRS COLLINS. Who, Kieran?

KIERAN. . . . Girls.

MALACHY. Aw, that's fascination.

KIERAN. No. And if you feel that, you have some responsibility afterwards.

MALACHY. Yeh?

KIERAN. I used to think – I'm not afraid to admit it – just giving her a kiss . . . A kiss: what's wrong with a kiss? That I wouldn't mind dying.

MALACHY. Aw, that's sex you're talking about, now.

KIERAN. What?

MALACHY. And a respectable married woman present – Even if she did marry a blow-in.

KIERAN. But what happens to it, where does it go?

MALACHY. Where are the snows of yesteryear, where have all the flowers gone, how much is that doggie in the window!

KIERAN. No. (*Indicating dancehall.*) Look at it! Look! Is this it?

MALACHY. Look, I've laid with more senoritas – saving your presence, Mrs Collins – than Don Juan and Valentino put together. (KIERAN *sighs at* MALACHY.) Right, I'll tell you what your problem is. Molly, you'll agree. Your trouble is as follows. Not only are you a romantic – like the poet Yeats – but, in my opinion, the famed Irish celibate personality has been imparted to you. Hold on! Look at it this way. From birth to the grave, Baptism to Extreme Unction there's always a celibate there somewhere, i.e., that is, a priest, a coonic. Teaching us in the schools, showing us how to play football, taking money at the ballroom doors, not to speak of preaching and officiating at the seven deadly sacraments.

MRS COLLINS. Malachy!

MALACHY. Wait on! And without any malice aforethought, as the fella said, the priest is imparting his attitude which is all very fine for him, but of no use to a fella like you with different aspirations. Do you follow me? Only a few of us escape.

Dance ends. He sees BRIDIE *and sucks in his breath.*

Who is she? The one with the hair and the – (*Figure.*)

MRS COLLINS. Isn't she one of the Ryans from Ahascragh side.

MALACHY. Is that who she is! – And the nuns – And the nuns nursing us in the hospitals in between. *And* doing our laundry for us. Think of that for a complication! No, wait a minute. They're all over the place. And what about the unemployment problem? What about that?

KIERAN. Stick to the point.

MRS COLLINS. You're a right Malachy!

MALACHY. I haven't worked a stroke in nearly four years.

KIERAN. No, no, a tangent!

MALACHY. How so?

KIERAN. What's unemployment got to do with it?

MALACHY. And who's got three-quarters of the jobs in the country? The celibates.

KIERAN. Tck!

MALACHY. And what about the black babies? The poor auld black babies: What about them? Dying in a state of barbaric paganism, and, *and*, for all we know, screaming African oaths when they could be saying the Hail Mary!

KIERAN. Ah, what's the use: you're worse than any of them.

MALACHY. I'm sticking to the point. You don't know about real sex at all yet.

KIERAN. Hah?

MALACHY (*watching* BRIDIE). Bow-wow! I want to make sure of nabbing her for this dance.

KIERAN. What?

MALACHY. What? What are you talking about?

KIERAN. What?

MALACHY. Wait'll you get the real thing.

KIERAN. What?

MALACHY. My soul to soar forevermore beside you Galway Bay! (*Another dance has started.*) Jasus, I've lost her again! That little fart!

WILLIE *has approached* BRIDIE *and is asking her to dance. She refuses. She comes towards soft drinks bar.*

KIERAN. No you haven't. (*Urging him.*) No you haven't. There you are.

MALACHY. Excuse me, as the fella said. Would you care to dance, Miss?

He leads her to the floor. They come together for the dance. After a moment she steps back from him, looking a little alarmed. He does not understand for a moment; then he remembers; mutters 'sorry', takes whiskey bottle from his trousers pocket and slips it into the side pocket of his jacket. They dance off.

MARGARET *is again standing on her own.* MR COLLINS, MISS D'ARCY *and* ANGELA *form a little circle of their own.* KIERAN *is working his way towards* MARGARET.

MISS D'ARCY. Oh, Kieran, Kieran! We were just talking about Shamie Mooney. You should see the dirt on his catechism today. Stand up, Shamie Mooney, I said. Now tell me why can't you have two wives. Miss, said he, you can't serve two masters.

MR COLLINS (*usual impassive face*). What? (*And walks away.*)

MISS D'ARCY. Miss, said he, you can't serve two masters.

KIERAN. Oh, he could be right too. (KIERAN – *a hard man* – gives MISS D'ARCY *a pat on the bottom as he leaves them.*)

WILLIE *beats* SEAN *to* ANGELA *and asks her to dance.* SEAN *is left with no choice but to ask* MISS D'ARCY.

MISS D'ARCY *and* SEAN *dance off.* KIERAN *is now standing beside* MARGARET.

KIERAN. Will you dance?

MARGARET. Thank you.

As they dance off:

KIERAN. . . . I heard of a teacher one time who asked the class one day, what are the two main churches in Ireland, and this little lad said . . .

MR COLLINS *and* MRS COLLINS *stand at the mineral bar, nothing to say to each other.*

WILLIE (*and* ANGELA *dance on*). Did anyone pay you in?

ANGELA. What?

WILLIE. Buy your ticket for you.

ANGELA. They did.

WILLIE. Any harm to ask who?

ANGELA. I did. (*They dance off.*)

MISS D'ARCY *and* SEAN *dance on, a gap between them;* SEAN *whistling, affecting a disinterested benevolence. They are followed by* MALACHY, *fancy-stepping, cheek-to-cheek, with* BRIDIE, *serenading her. They dance off.*

KIERAN *and* MARGARET *dance in.*

KIERAN. We got our backpay on Friday, backdated to the first of June. Which is alright, hmm?

MARGARET. I'm worried, Kieran.

KIERAN (*eyes dilated but trying to sound casual*). Hmm? . . . Hmm?

MARGARET. I'm worried. I didn't have – I'm worried.

KIERAN. And what are you worried about?

MARGARET. Things.

KIERAN. Things?

MARGARET. Things we shouldn't have done.

KIERAN. Hmm?

MARGARET. You know. You know. I'm worried.

KIERAN. Hmm?

MARGARET. Would you like to sit down?

KIERAN. Yes.

They are moving off the floor when MALACHY *and* BRIDIE *call them.*

MALACHY. Oh, Mr Morris! What time are your classes in the morning?

KIERAN. Half nine.

MALACHY. So are mine. Oh, this is Miss Ryan – Bridie – if you will pardon the familiarity.

BRIDIE. How do you do.

MALACHY. This is a colleague of mine, Mr Morris – Kieran, and Margaret Sweeney. We'll see you in a minute.

MALACHY *and* BRIDIE *return to their dancing.*

MARGARET. I don't like him.

KIERAN. Everyone is watching us.

They sit. Pause.

MARGARET. What are you thinking?

KIERAN. Ah . . . I was thinking about you.

MARGARET. . . . Good or bad?

KIERAN. Good . . . Ah . . . I met Connie what's-her-name – Connie thing the other day and she was asking for you.

MARGARET. Oh, did you?

KIERAN. I did.

MARGARET. Tell her I was asking for her if you see her again. . . . Hmm?

KIERAN. I will . . . How do you know?

MARGARET. I know. This is my time.

KIERAN. And when should you?

MARGARET. Few days ago. I think.

KIERAN. Aren't you sure? – Aren't you sure?

MARGARET *bows her head.*

. . . Because, as a matter of fact, I'm not sure if it was intercourse at all that we had that night! . . . You'll pull the nail off yourself picking at that chair! . . . But it was our first time!

MARGARET. I know.

KIERAN. . . . What?

MARGARET. I don't know how you can have any respect for me.

KIERAN. What?

MARGARET. You must hate me.

KIERAN. I've a good mind not to answer that.

MARGARET. Do you?

KIERAN. No.

MARGARET. Look at what I've brought you to.

KIERAN. What?

MARGARET. And after all the girls you ever went with.

KIERAN. I haven't gone with that many.

MARGARET. I wouldn't have wanted you to suffer because of it.

KIERAN. What do you mean: you wouldn't *have* wanted me to suffer?

MARGARET. . . . Oh Kieran! It isn't fair. (*His eyes scrutinizing her.*) . . . No, I'll go away and have . . . the child.

KIERAN. And the violins playing, I suppose, and the violins playing, I suppose, and the violins playing! Sure, it couldn't be definite yet! I know more about these matters than you think.

MALACHY *and* BRIDIE *join them.*

MALACHY. The square on the hypotenuse is equal to the sum of the squares on the other two sides! Are you enjoying yourselves? Bridie is home from Brum on holidays and I've invited her to take some libation. I think your bottle is open, Ciarán.

MALACHY *gets glasses from the soft drinks bar.*

BRIDIE. What have you got?

KIERAN (*shows her the bottle*). Are you enjoying the dance?

BRIDIE. Not really.

KIERAN. . . . How long have you been home?

BRIDIE. Eight days, like. I got fed up listening to mum and I thought I'd see what this jiggin's like. But quite honestly it's not my cup of tea. Know what I mean? (MALACHY *returns.*) But then it's very dull round here. Nothing ever happens round here.

MALACHY. Well, did you hear the one about your man who got the suit made and took it back to the tailor? This suit, said your man, is like the ballroom in Monivea. But there's no ballroom in Monivea, said the tailor. So you see what I mean said your man. (BRIDIE *laughs*.)
But seriously, Bridie, we were having a very serious and interesting discussion, my colleague and I, a while ago on the subject of, well, frankly, sex.

SEAN *joins them, eyeing* BRIDIE.

SEAN. How's it cutting?

MALACHY. Seán, Bridie, Bridie, Seán.

SEAN. How do you do, Bridie.

BRIDIE. I'm very well thank you, Seán.

SEAN. That's good.

MALACHY. But we were talking about this subject – Yeh know?

BRIDIE. You think it's all it's cracked up to be? Sex, like. I think it's cat, round here.

SEAN. . . . It's mouse.

MALACHY. My very point. Correct me if I'm wrong. But the whole idea of man and woman is a much bigger problem than people realize. Wouldn't you agree, Bridie?

BRIDIE. Ay?

WILLIE (*joining them*). Hello. Can I join you.

MALACHY. Bridie, Willie.

WILLIE. We've met. Bridie.

MALACHY. A much bigger problem. But do you know what the key is? Self-contempt is the metaphysical key. How can you, I ask myself, love someone, if, *if*, first, you do not love yourself. How can you do it? I will not mince words, as the fella said, with grown-up adults who know the score, but, but, to be frank, all those knee-trembling jobs – much as we enjoy them – And I'm not ruling them totally out – But all that kind of thing – Holy medals and genitalia in mortal combat with each other is not sex at all. Wouldn't you agree?

BRIDIE. Oh yes: all they do round here, all Irishmen do is talk about it.

MALACHY. Isn't that my point! For instance, Bridie, my mum and dad, unhappily have passed on, so I have a whole house all to myself. Do you see?

BRIDIE. Ay?

SEAN. Enjoying the dance, Bridie?

BRIDIE. It's alright like, Seán.

MALACHY. If you'd let me finish, Seán. No, all the aforementioned practices – coitus interruptus – coitus nonstartus! – not intercourse at all – if you'll pardon the expression. No. All that is indignity. But, *but*, what does the hypocritic intelligentia do? After all that indignity they go to the church, the fountain, to have their souls absolved. And the funny thing about it is, the poor auld soul has hump all to do with it, and the holy body is left with the sin against itself.

Music for the next dance has started.

KIERAN. I think the soul *has* something to do with it.

MALACHY (*turns to* KIERAN). Ay?

WILLIE ⎰
SEAN ⎱ Will you dance?

BRIDIE. Ta, Seán. Ta for the drink Malachy.

MALACHY. Keep the next one for me, Bridie.

She moves off with SEAN *for the dance.* WILLIE *is off immediately in search of someone else –* ANGELA. ANGELA *refuses* WILLIE's *request to dance with her: she comes to table.*

MALACHY. And you think the soul has something to do with it?

ANGELA. Hello.

KIERAN. Angela.

ANGELA. Enjoying yourself?

KIERAN. Yep.

FIRST MAN (*joining them*). Would you care to dance, miss?

ANGELA. Thank you. (*To* KIERAN.) See you. (*Moves off with* FIRST MAN.)

KIERAN (*to* MARGARET). Will you dance? (*To* MALACHY.) See you back here after the dance. (*They go to dance floor.*)

MARGARET. Who's Angela?

KIERAN. Oh, new teacher. Did I not tell you? (*They dance.*)

WILLIE *returns, not having found a partner.*

WILLIE. Who is she, what does she do, she wouldn't tell me: Bridie?

MALACHY. Will you go home and dry behind your ears, a mac. She's a nice sweet girl, home to visit her mum and dad, like, and you'd be no use to her at all.

WILLIE. There she is! Seán has her collared!

MALACHY. Not at all. I'm letting him do the footwork before I move in for the kill. Meanwhile . . . (*He looks around.*) I might do Miss D'Arcy the favour.

And WILLIE *is off like a shot to ask* MISS D'ARCY *to dance.* MISS D'ARCY *marches on to the dancefloor ahead of* WILLIE.

MR COLLINS *continues, still in his overcoat, at the soft drinks bar, beside his wife.*

MRS COLLINS (*absently: to herself*). The kids are all asleep by now.

MR COLLINS (*to himself*). Six bob was too pricey.

MALACHY (*calls to* KIERAN *and* MARGARET). There you are!

The following between KIERAN *and* MARGARET *as they dance.*

MARGARET. If this didn't happen, what would you do?

KIERAN. What do? What do you mean? We'll just have to behave better in future. That's all.

MARGARET. . . . Sorry. (*She starts to cry quietly.*)

KIERAN. What, Margaret?

MARGARET. I'm sorry.

KIERAN. Shh! . . . What are you crying for?

MARGARET. Oh, Kieran, Kieran!

KIERAN. Shh! – Don't – what are you – Aw, don't worry about it. Blue eyes. What are you crying for? I don't see how it can happen. Frankly. And even if it does, well it'll be alright too.

MARGARET. What?

KIERAN. Don't worry. I mean, don't be afraid of anything.

MARGARET. The only thing I'm afraid of is that you won't love me.

KIERAN. Oh, don't . . . I mean, I wouldn't worry about that.

MARGARET. What?

KIERAN. Don't worry about that.

MARGARET. What?

KIERAN. Yeh know.

MARGARET. Always?

KIERAN. Yeh . . . Yeh.

MARGARET. What?

KIERAN. Always. Forever and ever.

MARGARET. I don't care about anything else so . . . Sorry for this show I'm making of you. Dance me over towards the ladies. I'd better go in for a minute.

MARGARET *exits to ladies' cloakroom.*

KIERAN (*alone*). Jesus, what am I going to do?

He looks at the unhappy picture of MR COLLINS *and* MRS COL-LINS.

MR COLLINS. Are you on your ear?

KIERAN. No.

MR COLLINS. Be in on time now in the morning. (KIERAN *nods.*) . . . I don't like coming out at all . . . Only upsetting myself. (*He winks at* KIERAN – *same serious face.*)

MALACHY (*joining them*). Well, he's a terrible pig of a man.

MR COLLINS. Yeh, he's a terrible animal.

KIERAN (*laughs, a touch of hysteria in it. To* MRS COLLINS). I'll be going home. See you. (*Exits.*)

MALACHY. We can all relax now.

KIERAN *finishes his quarter bottle, then laughs suddenly again.*

KIERAN. Do you . . . do you trust women, Malachy?

MALACHY. A strange mixture, Ciarán, of cunning and innocence. And like Aristotle, I don't mind admitting I don't follow them completely.

KIERAN. I'd love to be free.

MALACHY. Wouldn't we all!

KIERAN. No, I mean – FREE! Free, free! Out fast, a quick powder. And I had my chances.

MALACHY. The quare one, is it? (*MARGARET*)

KIERAN. No. No, she's – she's sound. (*Sings.*) Oh you can rock it, you can roll it, you can take it out and hold it at the hop!

MALACHY. You can wank it, you can spank it, you can welt it, you can belt it at the hop!

KIERAN
MALACHY } Let's go to the hop! (etc.)

KIERAN. Like, if misfortune wants to single me out, well hump misfortune. That's all!

MALACHY. You can ease it, you can tease it –

KIERAN. Every little plan I ever had gone arseways! –

MALACHY. You can squeeze it, you can please it, at the hop!

KIERAN. I got a horse! Hear ye, hear ye!

MALACHY. Let's go to the hop! . . .

KIERAN. Listen, Malachy – listen friends! If all were known, I'm probably the hardest man of all times. Listen, friends! Listen everybody! I've had sex – Not my oats! Sex! Sex! Sex! Sex! I've had it, the real thing. Often. Many's the time.

MALACHY. Many's the time and oft, behind the Rialto!

KIERAN. No! Not behind any place. Not in a car, a doorway, or furnace room, or lavatory, or lavatory – !

MALACHY. Easy, take it easy.

KIERAN. And I'm proud to say I had my clothes off!

MALACHY. What's up with you? Margaret is it?

KIERAN. What? I didn't say that. I don't talk about women like that.

MALACHY. You're talking generally.

KIERAN. I'm talking – generally. I'm talking about sex.

MALACHY. And your soul has something to do with it?

KIERAN. What? Yes . . . Yes.

MALACHY. Oh to think of it, oh, to dream of it, fills my heart with tears!

KIERAN (quietly). Yes.

MARGARET comes out of cloakroom and stands on edge of dance floor. She does not see them.

KIERAN (to himself). Oh, Margaret.

MALACHY. I'd abandon her if I were you.

KIERAN (quietly). It must be the hardest thing in the world – to smile when you can't. One time, effortless. But the night we met . . . Malachy?

MALACHY. I'm listening.

KIERAN. I nodded across the hall to her. And she cocked her head to one side, and nodded back. And my hand to her waist for the dance. And I couldn't believe it. So slender. And she's big, But it kept sinking. So slender. I never knew about a woman's waist before. Yeh know. The other things are obvious . . . So slender. But frail. . . . And later on – Malachy? – she told me she'd been watching me too.

MALACHY. I think Seán has collared Bridie alright.

KIERAN. What? No. No, look she's looking this way.

MALACHY. I don't think so. I think I put myself out of her reach by granting myself a teacher's diploma.

KIERAN. . . . But wouldn't you say that Margaret is as goodlooking as any average – No. not average. She's as goodlooking as any woman going. What more can a man expect? And of course I like her – Love her. Love her – no matter what I say myself.

MALACHY. The job's a good one.

KIERAN. And she comes from nice people. Sure her mother is a lovely woman. And she likes me. And I like her mother. And her fath – Well, he's a bit of an eejit. The dead eyes of the man. He should take more interest. And listen to this.

MALACHY. I'm listening.

KIERAN. Supposing it was that Agnes Murphy I was in-in-volved with now. Wouldn't that be a nice thing? Granted, Agnes is a lovely dancer, but, my God, she looks like a thin sheep. Think of that when you want to know how lucky you are.

MALACHY. Count your blessings, boy.

KIERAN. What? And what kind of a job is teaching anyway? When you're slave-driven. Four hundred and two pounds a year! And it's so dead, so dead around here. Everyone should see a bit of the world. And do you know what's wrong? Celibate personality. Do you want a celibate personality? I don't want a celibate personality. But that's what they've given me. To welter for years in guilt and indignity. How can you win? I'm getting away from it all.

MALACHY. What? What are you rambling on about?

KIERAN. Away! There's nothing happening here.

MALACHY. England?

KIERAN. . . . No . . . Canada. It's different there.

MALACHY. Wait for the grey morning light, Ciarán.

KIERAN. No. No more of it. Look: Look at her: sure she's the loveliest little girl you ever clapped an eye on. Things are looking up.

Dance ends. MISS D'ARCY, *followed by* WILLIE, *comes off the floor.*

MISS D'ARCY. Christ's sake, you're like an octopus!

WILLIE *continues on to* MARGARET.

WILLIE. Will you dance the next one with me?

MARGARET (*sees* KIERAN *approaching*). Sorry.

SEAN *is talking earnestly to* BRIDIE. KIERAN *joins* MAR-GARET.

MALACHY *exits to gents.*

MARGARET (*laughs*). You're drunk!

KIERAN (*does a few steps to demonstrate his agile sobriety*). No! I have it, Mar. Things are looking up. How would you like to go to Canada? No more cold nights. Evacuation stakes . . . Hmm? What's the matter.

MARGARET. I was telling lies. Not completely. I believed I was. I was sure of it, honestly, all the week. I wanted to be, and I went to the doctor yesterday, and he said, 'not by any stretch of the imagination'. I thought it was so unfair . . . It would have killed mammy.

KIERAN. I mostly worried about your mother too.

MARGARET. Your job, and my mother . . . You're happy now.

KIERAN. Hmm?

MARGARET. You're happy now it's off your mind.

KIERAN (*absently*). Yeh. I feel a sort of form of disappointment.

MARGARET. That's the way I feel.

They look at each other and smile sadly.

Anyway, I wouldn't want any man to marry me because he had to.

KIERAN. Any man! I thought we'd talked about all that one night.

She smiles, frankly pleased. He kisses her.

MARGARET. That was nice.

KIERAN. Fat belly.

MARGARET. Oh my love I love you so much.

KIERAN. I love you too.

They laugh delighted. Then she becomes serious.

MARGARET. Do you?

He nods. They laugh again. Now an idea forming – a tacit understanding in it.

KIERAN. Will you come somewhere, with me?

She nods.

Not the usual places. Malachy has a house all to himself. He might give me the key. (*She nods her agreement.*) We'll do it right this time. (*She nods.*) Get your coat.

MARGARET. Alright. (*She exits.*)

KIERAN *is looking around for* MALACHY.

MISS D'ARCY. Well, you're an awful man for patting women's bottoms!

KIERAN. Excuse me.

He gets away from her. FIRST MAN *is taking* ANGELA *to soft drinks bar.* MALACHY *emerges from gents, singing an Elvis number and, as he passes by* SEAN *and* BRIDIE:

MALACHY (*to* SEAN). Louser!

BRIDIE. Ta-ta, Seán. (*She follows* MALACHY.)

MALACHY (*singing to himself*). 'Oh what a night it was, oh what a night it was, it really was such a night.'

BRIDIE. Coo, it isn't half hot in here. Well, will we go? . . . Back to your house.

MALACHY. . . . I'm squared – Another lady – You didn't give me enough notice.

BRIDIE *walks away.* KIERAN *comes up to him.*

KIERAN. Will you give us the key to the house?

MALACHY. Is that the way it is. (*Gives key.*) First left, top of the stairs. Leave the key over the door. I'm going to give it a miss for a change tonight.

KIERAN. Thanks.

MARGARET *comes out of cloakroom with her overcoat and exits.* KIERAN *salutes* MALACHY *as he exits a moment later.*

Band starts playing the next dance. MALACHY *surveys the scene:* FIRST MAN *leading* ANGELA *on to dancefloor;* MISS D'ARCY *on her own;* MRS COLLINS *laughing;* WILLIE *biting his nails wondering which way to run next.*

MALACHY *takes out his quarter bottle of whiskey which he has managed to preserve intact all night: he contemplates the quarter bottle:*

MALACHY. What is this thing called love?

He drinks.

1. Feb . 06 Midwest 28 15 975 7/

Printed in the United States
40668LVS00001B/147